CAKES, BAKES and BISCUITS

Nothing beats the taste of home-baked cakes and biscuits. Today many people think of home-baked goodies as nothing more than a delightful memory. This need not be so. This book will show that not only is baking an easy and affordable way to fill lunch boxes and provide snacks for your family but it is also fun.

Here you will find a host of recipes that are easy to make and will bring those distant memories back to life. So turn the pages, select your recipe and start baking again.

THE PANTRY SHELF
Unless otherwise stated, the following ingredients used in this book are:
Cream   Double, suitable for whipping
Flour   White flour, plain or standard
Sugar   White sugar

WHAT'S IN A TABLESPOON?
NEW ZEALAND
1 tablespoon =
15 mL OR 3 teaspoons
UNITED KINGDOM
1 tablespoon =
15 mL OR 3 teaspoons
AUSTRALIA
1 tablespoon =
20 mL OR 4 teaspoons
The recipes in this book were tested in Australia where a 20 mL tablespoon is standard. All measures are level.

The tablespoon in the New Zealand and United Kingdom sets of measuring spoons is 15 mL. In many recipes this difference will not matter. For recipes using baking powder, gelatine, bicarbonate of soda, small quantities of flour and cornflour, simply add another teaspoon for each tablespoon specified.

CONTENTS

SPONGES

*Quick to prepare and cook and as light as air, a sponge cake is
hard to resist. Remember that sponges do not keep well, so are
best made on the day that you intend to eat them.*

Coffee Sandwich Cake

COFFEE SANDWICH CAKE

250 g/8 oz butter, softened
1 cup/220 g/7 oz caster sugar
6 eggs, lightly beaten
2 cups/250 g/8 oz self-raising
flour, sifted
4 teaspoons baking powder

COFFEE ICING
60 g/2 oz butter, softened
^{3}/4 cup/125 g/4 oz icing sugar, sifted
^{1}/2 teaspoon ground cinnamon
2 teaspoons instant coffee powder
dissolved in 2 teaspoons
hot water, cooled

LIQUEUR CREAM
1 tablespoon coffee-flavoured liqueur
^{1}/2 cup/125 mL/4 fl oz cream (double),
whipped

1 Place butter and sugar in a food processor and process until creamy. Add eggs, flour and baking powder and process until all ingredients are combined. Spoon batter into two greased and lined 18 cm/7 in sandwich tins and bake for 30-35 minutes or until golden and cooked when tested with a skewer. Turn cakes onto wire racks to cool.

2 To make icing, place butter, icing sugar, cinnamon and coffee mixture in a food processor and process until light and fluffy.

3 To make filling, fold liqueur into whipped cream. Spread filling over one cake and top with remaining cake. Spread icing over top of cake.

Makes an 18 cm/7 in sandwich cake

Oven temperature
160°C, 325°F, Gas 3

For a nonalcoholic filling, dissolve 1 teaspoon instant coffee powder in 1 teaspoon hot water. Cool, then fold into cream.

SWISS ROLL

4 eggs
^{1}/2 cup/100 g/3^1/2 oz caster sugar
1 cup/125 g/4 oz self-raising flour
^{1}/3 cup/90 mL/3 fl oz hot milk
^{1}/2 cup/125 mL/4 fl oz cream (double),
whipped (optional)
125 g/4 oz strawberries, sliced,
or 2 tablespoons raspberry jam
icing sugar, sifted

1 Place eggs and sugar in a bowl and beat until thick and creamy.

2 Sift flour three times and fold into egg mixture. Fold milk into batter and pour into a greased and lined 26 x 32 cm/10^1/2

x 12^3/4 in Swiss roll tin and bake for 20-25 minutes or until sponge springs back when touched with the fingertips.

3 Turn sponge onto a damp teatowel sprinkled with caster sugar. Carefully remove lining paper from sponge and carefully roll up from short end. Set aside to cool completely.

4 Unroll sponge, spread with whipped cream, if used, top with strawberries, reroll, sprinkle with icing sugar and serve. Alternatively, the sponge can be spread with raspberry jam and cream or just with raspberry jam.

Serves 8-10

Oven temperature
190°C, 375°F, Gas 5

When making a whisked sponge such as this one, you need to beat the egg mixture until it is thick and creamy. This will take 8-10 minutes using an electric mixer. At the completion of beating, a thick ribbon trail will be left when the beaters are lifted from the mixture.

LAMINGTONS

Oven temperature
180°C, 350°F, Gas 4

125 g/4 oz butter
$^3/4$ cup/170 g/5$^1/2$ oz caster sugar
1 teaspoon vanilla essence
2 eggs
1 cup/125 g/4 oz flour
1 cup/125 g/4 oz self-raising flour
1 teaspoon baking powder
$^1/2$ cup/125 mL/4 fl oz milk

CHOCOLATE ICING
3 cups/500 g/1 lb icing sugar, sifted
3$^1/2$ tablespoons cocoa powder, sifted
6-8 tablespoons boiling water
desiccated coconut

To make coating the cake easier, place coconut and icing in two shallow dishes or cake tins. Use tongs or two forks to dip the cake in the icing, then place on a wire rack set over a sheet of paper and allow to drain for 2-3 minutes before rolling in the coconut.

1 Place butter, sugar and vanilla essence in a bowl and beat until light and fluffy. Beat in eggs one at a time, beating well after each addition.

2 Sift together flour, self-raising flour and baking powder. Fold flour mixture and milk, alternately, into butter mixture. Pour batter into a greased and lined 26 x 32 cm/10$^1/2$ x 12$^3/4$ in Swiss roll tin and bake for 30-35 minutes or until sponge springs back when touched with the fingertips. Allow cake to stand in tin for 5 minutes before turning onto a wire rack to cool completely.

3 To make icing, sift icing sugar and cocoa powder together into a large bowl and mix in sufficient water to make an icing with a smooth, coating consistency.

4 Cut cake into twelve squares. Dip each piece of cake in chocolate icing to completely coat, then roll in coconut and place on nonstick baking paper to set.

Makes 12

Left: Lamingtons
Below: Victoria Sponge

VICTORIA SPONGE

250 g/8 oz butter
1 cup/220 g/7 oz caster sugar
1 teaspoon vanilla essence
4 eggs, lightly beaten
2 cups/250 g/8 oz self-raising flour
pinch salt
icing sugar, sifted

FILLING
3 tablespoons strawberry or
raspberry jam
$^1/_2$ cup/125 mL/4 fl oz cream (double),
whipped

1 Place butter, sugar and vanilla essence in a bowl and beat until light and fluffy. Slowly add eggs, beating well after each addition.

2 Sift together flour and salt and fold into egg mixture. Spoon batter into two greased and lined 20 cm/8 in sandwich tins and bake for 30-35 minutes or until sponge springs back when touched with the fingertips. Allow cakes to stand in tins for 2 minutes before turning onto wire racks to cool completely.

3 Spread one sponge with jam, top with whipped cream and other cake. Dust top of cake with icing sugar.

Makes a 20 cm/8 in sandwich cake

Oven temperature
190°C, 375°F, Gas 5

If eggs are added too quickly to a creamed mixture, the mixture will curdle. If curdling occurs, fold in a little of the flour used in the recipe, then continue beating in the eggs.

MOCHA SPONGE

Oven temperature
190°C, 375°F, Gas 5

3 eggs, separated
$^1/2$ cup/100 g/3$^1/2$ oz caster sugar
$^3/4$ cup/90 g/3 oz self-raising flour
pinch salt
1 tablespoon cocoa powder
1 teaspoon melted butter
1 teaspoon instant coffee powder
2 tablespoons boiling water

COFFEE CREAM FILLING
1 tablespoon instant coffee powder
1 tablespoon hot milk
$^1/2$ cup/125 mL/4 fl oz cream (double),
whipped
1-2 tablespoons icing sugar, sifted

GLACE ICING
1 cup/155 g/5 oz icing sugar, sifted
1 tablespoon boiling water
15 g/$^1/2$ oz butter
$^1/4$ teaspoon vanilla essence
1 tablespoon caramel ice cream topping
2 teaspoons instant coffee powder

1   Place egg whites in a bowl and beat until stiff peaks form. Gradually add sugar, beating well after each addition, until mixture is thick and glossy. Add egg yolks one at a time, beating well after each addition.

2   Sift together flour, salt and cocoa powder, then sift mixture twice more. Fold flour mixture into egg mixture. Combine butter, instant coffee powder and boiling water and pour around the edge of the batter, then fold in using a metal spoon.

3   Pour batter into two greased and lined 18 cm/7 in sandwich tins and bake for 20-25 minutes or until sponge springs back when touched with the fingertips. Allow cakes to stand in tins for 3-4 minutes before turning onto wire racks to cool completely.

4   To make filling, dissolve instant coffee powder in milk and fold into whipped cream. Sweeten to taste with icing sugar. Spread one cake with filling, then top with other cake.

5   To make icing, place icing sugar in a heatproof bowl, set over a saucepan of simmering water. Make a well in the centre of the icing sugar, add boiling water, butter and vanilla essence and cook, stirring slowly, until mixture is smooth and shiny. Pour half the mixture into a separate bowl and stir in the caramel topping. Stir instant coffee powder into remaining mixture.

6   Spread top of cake with caramel-flavoured icing. Then, while the icing is still warm, place the coffee-flavoured icing in a plastic food bag, snip off the corner and pipe parallel lines, 2 cm/$^3/4$ in apart, across the top of the cake. Using a metal skewer, lightly draw across the lines at 2 cm/$^3/4$ in intervals in the opposite direction, to give a feathered effect.

Makes an 18 cm/7 in sandwich cake

When making a sponge cake, sift the dry ingredients three times to incorporate air into the mixture. This helps to ensure a light-as-air cake.

Chocolate Roll

CHOCOLATE ROLL

5 eggs, separated
$^1/_4$ cup/60 g/2 oz caster sugar
100 g/$3^1/_2$ oz dark chocolate, melted
and cooled
2 tablespoons self-raising flour, sifted
with 2 tablespoons cocoa powder

CHOCOLATE FILLING
60 g/2 oz dark chocolate
$^2/_3$ cup/170 mL/$5^1/_2$ fl oz cream
(double)

1 Place egg yolks and sugar in a mixing bowl and beat until mixture is thick and creamy. Beat in chocolate, then fold in flour mixture.

2 Place egg whites in a clean bowl and beat until stiff peaks form. Fold egg white mixture into chocolate mixture. Pour batter into a greased and lined 26 x 32 cm/ $10^1/_2$ x $12^3/_4$ in Swiss roll tin and bake for 12-15 minutes or until sponge springs back when touched with the fingertips. Turn onto a damp teatowel sprinkled with caster sugar. Carefully remove lining paper from sponge and carefully roll up from short end. Set aside to cool completely.

3 To make filling, place chocolate and cream in a small saucepan and cook over a low heat, stirring, until chocolate melts and mixture is well blended. Bring to the boil, remove from heat and set aside to cool completely. When cold, place in a mixing bowl set over ice and beat until thick and creamy.

4 Unroll cake, spread with filling and reroll. To serve, cut into slices.

Serves 8

Oven temperature
180°C, 350°F, Gas 4

Always test a whisked sponge by lightly touching the top of it – when it is cooked the cake will spring back. Do not use a skewer to test this type of cake as this can cause it to sink in the middle.

COOKIES & SLICES

In this chapter you will find a wonderful array of cookies, biscuits and slices. It is easy to understand why this type of baked product is popular. Not only are they easy to make, but they come in a huge variety of flavours and textures. Best of all, they are just the right size for a snack.

Coconut Cookies

125 g/4 oz butter, chopped
1 cup/170 g/5$^1/2$ oz brown sugar
1 teaspoon vanilla essence
1 egg
1 cup/125 g/4 oz flour
$^1/2$ cup/60 g/2 oz self-raising flour
1 cup/90 g/3 oz rolled oats
45 g/1$^1/2$ oz desiccated coconut
2 teaspoons finely grated lime rind
2 tablespoons lime juice

1   Place butter, sugar, vanilla essence, egg, flour, self-raising flour, rolled oats, coconut, lime rind and lime juice in a food processor and process until well combined.

2   Drop heaped teaspoons of mixture on greased baking trays and bake for 12-15 minutes or until lightly browned. Transfer to wire racks to cool.

Makes 35

Oven temperature
180°C, 350°F, Gas 4

The tang of lime and the unique flavour and texture of coconut combine to make these wonderful cookies.

Golden Oat Biscuits

1 cup/90 g/3 oz rolled oats
1 cup/125 g/4 oz flour, sifted
90 g/3 oz desiccated coconut
1 cup/250 g/8 oz sugar
4 teaspoons golden syrup, warmed
125 g/4 oz butter, melted
2 tablespoons boiling water
1 teaspoon bicarbonate of soda

1   Place rolled oats, flour, coconut and sugar in a large bowl. Combine golden syrup, butter, water and bicarbonate of soda.

2   Pour golden syrup mixture into dry ingredients and mix well to combine. Drop teaspoons of mixture 3 cm/1$^1/4$ in apart on greased baking trays and bake for 10-15 minutes or until biscuits are just firm. Stand on trays for 3 minutes before transferring to wire racks to cool.

Makes 30

Oven temperature
180°C, 350°F, Gas 4

Biscuits should always be stored in an airtight container. Allow the biscuits to cool completely on wire cooling racks before storing.

Coconut Cookies, Golden Oat Biscuits

Honey Malt Bars

Oven temperature
180°C, 350°F, Gas 4

The easiest way to cut a slice into even pieces is to cut it in half lengthwise, then to cut each half in half, again lengthwise. Then cut the slice in half in the opposite direction and cut each half into thirds. This method of cutting the slice can be varied according to the size and shape you want your pieces to be. For example, for fingers or bars, instead of cutting into thirds at the final stage only cut in half again.

2 cups/250 g/8 oz self-raising
flour, sifted
1 cup/90 g/3 oz rolled oats
90 g/3 oz desiccated coconut
250 g/8 oz crushed Weet-Bix
(Weetabix)
1 cup/170 g/5^1/$_2$ oz brown sugar
250 g/8 oz butter, melted
4 tablespoons honey

MOCHA ICING
1 cup/155 g/5 oz icing sugar
2 teaspoons cocoa powder
2 teaspoons instant coffee powder
15 g/^{1}/$_2$ oz butter, softened
1-2 tablespoons water

1   Place flour, rolled oats, coconut, Weet-Bix (Weetabix) and sugar in a large bowl and mix well to combine. Combine butter and honey and stir into dry ingredients.

2   Press mixture into a greased and lined 18 x 26 cm/7 x 10^1/$_2$ in shallow cake tin and bake for 35-40 minutes or until golden brown. Allow to cool in tin.

3   To make icing, sift icing sugar, cocoa powder and instant coffee powder together into a heatproof bowl. Add butter, stir in water and mix to a stiff consistency. Place bowl over a saucepan of simmering water and heat, stirring constantly, to make an icing of spreading consistency. Spread icing over slice. Allow icing to set and cut slice into bars.

Makes 20 bars

Sesame Fruit Fingers

Oven temperature
180°C, 350°F, Gas 4

Remember when making any baked product that the oven must be preheated before you put the cake, biscuit or slice in to cook.

185 g/6 oz untoasted muesli
60 g/2 oz desiccated coconut
^{1}/$_2$ cup/75 g/2^1/$_2$ oz wholemeal flour,
sifted and husks returned
60 g/2 oz pine nuts
125 g/4 oz sultanas
3 tablespoons sesame seeds
^{1}/$_2$ cup/90 g/3 oz brown sugar
125 g/4 oz butter, melted and cooled
2 tablespoons golden syrup
2 eggs, lightly beaten

1   Place muesli, coconut, flour, pine nuts, sultanas, sesame seeds and sugar in a bowl and mix to combine. Combine butter, golden syrup and eggs and stir into dry ingredients.

2   Press mixture into a greased and lined 18 x 26 cm/7 x 10^1/$_2$ in shallow cake tin and bake for 20-25 minutes. Cool in tin and cut into fingers.

Makes 20

Honey Malt Bars, Hazelnut Fingers, Orange
Shortbread, Sesame Fruit Fingers, Almond
Cookies, Choc-Chip Cookies

ALMOND COOKIES

Oven temperature
180°C, 350°F, Gas 4

Biscuits, cookies and slices
make great gifts. Not only
are they economical but you
can make them to suit the
tastes of whoever you are
giving them to.
For the baked product to
stay fresh, remember that the
container you choose should
be airtight. If it isn't, wrap the
biscuits, cookies or slices in
plastic food wrap or seal in
cellophane bags. It is also a
nice idea to include the
recipe with your gift.

125 g/4 oz butter
1 cup/220 g/7 oz caster sugar
^{1}/2 teaspoon almond essence
1 egg
1 cup/125 g/4 oz flour, sifted
1 cup/125 g/4 oz self-raising flour, sifted
45 g/1^1/2 oz desiccated coconut
90 g/3 oz glacé cherries, chopped
125 g/4 oz chopped almonds

1   Place butter and sugar in a bowl and
beat until light and fluffy. Beat in almond
essence and egg, then fold in flour, self-
raising flour, coconut and cherries. Cover
and refrigerate for 2 hours.

2   Roll heaped teaspoons of mixture into
balls. Dip one half of each ball in
chopped almonds and arrange almond
side up on greased baking trays, spacing
balls well apart. Flatten each ball slightly
and bake for 12-15 minutes or until
golden. Remove to wire racks to cool
completely.

Makes 36

HAZELNUT FINGERS

Oven temperature
180°C, 350°F, Gas 4

The consistency of ground
nuts is important to the
success of a recipe. Ground
nuts should be a powder not
a paste. Particular care
should be taken when using
a food processor or grinder
as these appliances chop
nuts very quickly. When
chopping or grinding nuts in
a food processor use the
pulse button and only chop
about 60 g/2 oz at one time.
A little of the sugar or flour
used in the recipe added to
the nuts will help avoid
overprocessing.

3 egg whites
^{3}/4 cup/170 g/5^1/2 oz caster sugar
250 g/8 oz ground hazelnuts
^{1}/2 teaspoon almond essence
3 tablespoons cornflour, sifted
3 tablespoons flour, sifted
100 g/3^1/2 oz dark chocolate, melted

1   Place egg whites in a bowl and beat
until soft peaks form. Gradually add sugar,
beating well after each addition, until
mixture is thick and glossy.

2   Fold hazelnuts, almond essence,
cornflour and flour into egg white
mixture. Spoon mixture into a piping bag
fitted with a large plain nozzle, and pipe
5 cm/2 in lengths of mixture onto greased
baking trays, then bake for 10 minutes.
Remove to wire racks to cool completely.

3   Dip biscuit ends in melted chocolate
and place on aluminium foil to set.

Makes 45

Fig Pinwheels

FIG PINWHEELS

170 g/5¹/₂ oz butter
1 cup/170 g/5¹/₂ oz brown sugar
1 egg
¹/₂ teaspoon vanilla essence
3 cups/375 g/12 oz flour
¹/₂ teaspoon bicarbonate of soda
¹/₄ teaspoon ground cinnamon
¹/₄ teaspoon ground nutmeg
2 tablespoons milk

FIG AND ALMOND FILLING
250 g/8 oz dried figs, finely chopped
¹/₄ cup/60 g/2 oz sugar
¹/₂ cup/125 mL/4 fl oz water
¹/₄ teaspoon ground mixed spice
30 g/1 oz almonds, finely chopped

1 To make filling, place figs, sugar, water and mixed spice in a saucepan and bring to the boil. Reduce heat and cook, stirring, for 2-3 minutes or until mixture is thick. Remove pan from heat and stir in almonds. Set aside to cool.

2 Place butter in a bowl and beat until light and fluffy. Gradually add sugar, beating well after each addition until mixture is creamy. Beat in egg and vanilla essence.

3 Sift together flour, bicarbonate of soda, cinnamon and nutmeg. Beat milk and half the flour mixture into butter mixture. Stir in remaining flour mixture. Turn dough onto a lightly floured surface and knead briefly. Roll into a ball, wrap in plastic food wrap and refrigerate for 30 minutes.

4 Divide dough into two portions. Roll one portion out to a 20 x 28 cm/8 x 11 in rectangle and spread with half the filling. Roll up like a Swiss roll from the long side. Repeat with remaining dough and filling. Wrap rolls in plastic food wrap and refrigerate for 15 minutes or until you are ready to cook the biscuits.

5 Cut rolls into 1 cm/¹/₂ in slices. Place slices on lightly greased baking trays and bake for 10-12 minutes. Stand biscuits on trays for 1 minute before removing to wire racks to cool completely.

Makes 50

Oven temperature
180°C, 350°F, Gas 4

The uncooked rolls can be frozen if you wish. When you have unexpected guests, or the biscuit barrel is empty, these biscuits are great standbys.

CHOC-CHIP COOKIES

If you do not have chocolate chips, you can make these biscuits using roughly chopped chocolate instead. For something different you might like to use white chocolate or a mixture of dark and white chocolate.

125 g/4 oz butter
$^1/_2$ cup/100 g/3$^1/_2$ oz caster sugar
$^1/_2$ cup/90 g/3 oz brown sugar
1 egg
$^3/_4$ cup/90 g/3 oz flour, sifted
60 g/2 oz desiccated coconut
125 g/4 oz chocolate chips
100 g/3$^1/_2$ oz dark chocolate, melted
and cooled

1 Place butter, caster sugar and brown sugar in a bowl and beat until light and fluffy. Beat in egg, then fold in flour, coconut and chocolate chips.

2 Drop teaspoons of mixture on greased baking trays, allowing room for spreading, and bake for 15 minutes. Remove to wire racks to cool completely.

3 Place melted chocolate in a plastic food bag, snip off corner and pipe three lines across the top of each cookie.

Makes 36

ORANGE SHORTBREAD

250 g/8 oz butter
$^1/_2$ cup/100 g/3$^1/_2$ oz caster sugar
plus 1 tablespoon
3 teaspoons orange juice
1 teaspoon finely grated orange rind
2 cups/250 g/8 oz flour
$^1/_2$ cup/60 g/2 oz cornflour

1 Place butter and $^1/_2$ cup/125 g/4 oz sugar in a bowl and beat until light and fluffy. Beat in orange juice and orange rind. Sift together flour and cornflour and fold into butter mixture.

2 Press mixture into a greased and lined 20 cm/8 in square cake tin. Mark into squares, prick with a fork, sprinkle with remaining caster sugar and bake for 40-45 minutes or until just golden. Allow to cool in tin, then cut into squares.

Makes 20 squares

Coffee Kisses

COFFEE KISSES

250 g/8 oz butter, softened
^{2}/3 cup/100 g/3^1/2 oz icing sugar, sifted
2 teaspoons instant coffee powder
dissolved in 1 tablespoon hot
water, cooled
2 cups/250 g/8 oz flour, sifted
45 g/1^1/2 oz dark chocolate, melted
icing sugar

1   Place butter and icing sugar in a bowl and beat until light and fluffy. Stir in coffee mixture and flour.

2   Spoon mixture into a piping bag fitted with a medium star nozzle and pipe 2 cm/^{3}/4 in rounds of mixture 2 cm/^{3}/4 in apart on greased baking trays. Bake for 10-12 minutes or until lightly browned. Stand on trays for 5 minutes before removing to wire racks to cool completely.

3   Join biscuits with a little melted chocolate, then dust with icing sugar.

Makes 25

Oven temperature
180°C, 350°F, Gas 4

These coffee-flavoured biscuits have a similar texture to shortbread – making the dough perfect for piping. For something different you might like to pipe 5 cm/2 in lengths instead of rounds. Rather than sandwiching the biscuits together with chocolate you might prefer to leave them plain and simply dusted with icing sugar.

AFGHAN BISCUITS

Oven temperature
200°C, 400°F, Gas 6

200 g/6^1/2 oz butter, softened
1 teaspoon vanilla essence
^{1}/2 cup/100 g/3^1/2 oz caster sugar
1^1/2 cups/185 g/6 oz flour
1 teaspoon baking powder
1 tablespoon cocoa powder
90 g/3 oz cornflakes, crushed
2 tablespoons chopped sultanas
slivered almonds

CHOCOLATE ICING
15 g/^{1}/2 oz butter, softened
1 tablespoon cocoa powder
1 cup/155 g/5 oz icing sugar, sifted
1 tablespoon boiling water

1 Place butter and vanilla essence in a bowl and beat until light and fluffy. Gradually add sugar, beating well after each addition until mixture is creamy.

2 Sift together flour, baking powder and cocoa powder. Stir flour mixture into butter mixture, then fold in cornflakes and sultanas. Drop heaped teaspoons of mixture onto greased baking trays and bake for 12-15 minutes. Remove to wire racks to cool completely.

3 To make icing, place butter, cocoa powder and icing sugar in a bowl and mix with enough water to make an icing of spreading consistency.

4 Place a little icing on each biscuit and sprinkle with almonds. Set aside until icing firms.

Makes 30

Do not store different types of biscuits together as they absorb flavour and moisture from each other.

MELTING MOMENTS

Oven temperature
180°C, 350°F, Gas 4

250 g/8 oz butter, softened
4 tablespoons icing sugar, sifted
1 cup/125 g/4 oz cornflour
1 cup/125 g/4 oz flour

LEMON CREAM FILLING
60 g/2 oz butter, softened
^{1}/2 cup/75 g/2^1/2 oz icing sugar
2 teaspoons finely grated lemon rind
1 tablespoon lemon juice

1 Place butter and icing sugar in a bowl and beat until light and fluffy. Sift together cornflour and flour and stir into butter mixture.

2 Spoon mixture into a piping bag fitted with a large star nozzle and pipe small rosettes on greased baking trays, leaving space between each rosette. Bake for 15-20 minutes or until just golden. Allow biscuits to cool on trays.

3 To make filling, place butter in a bowl and beat until light and fluffy. Gradually add icing sugar and beat until creamy. Stir in lemon rind and lemon juice. Sandwich biscuits together with filling.

Makes 24

Grease baking trays with a little vegetable oil. Biscuits should be of a uniform size; not only will they look more attractive but they will also cook more evenly.

GINGER SNAPS

1 cup/170 g/5^1/$_2$ oz brown sugar
3 teaspoons ground ginger
2 cups/250 g/8 oz flour
125 g/4 oz butter
1 cup/350 g/11 oz golden syrup
1 teaspoon bicarbonate of soda

1   Sift brown sugar, ginger and flour together into a bowl.

2   Place butter and golden syrup in a saucepan and cook over a low heat, stirring, until butter melts. Stir in bicarbonate of soda. Pour golden syrup mixture into dry ingredients and mix until smooth.

3   Drop teaspoons of mixture onto greased baking trays and bake for 10-12 minutes or until golden. Remove from oven, loosen biscuits with a spatula and allow to cool on trays.

Oven temperature
180°C, 350°F, Gas 4

As these biscuits cool they become crisp.

Afghan Biscuits, Melting Moments, Ginger Snaps   **Makes 45**

CHRISTMAS COOKIES

Oven temperature
180°C, 350°F, Gas 4

125 g/4 oz butter
1 cup/220 g/7 oz caster sugar
1 egg, lightly beaten
2 teaspoons vanilla essence
$^1/_4$ cup/60 mL/2 fl oz milk
1$^1/_4$ cups/155 g/5 oz flour
$^1/_2$ teaspoon bicarbonate of soda
90 g/3 oz roasted hazelnuts, chopped
125 g/4 oz chocolate chips
90 g/3 oz shredded coconut
90 g/3 oz sultanas
90 g/3 oz glacé cherries, chopped

1 Place butter and sugar in a bowl and beat until light and fluffy. Beat in egg, vanilla essence and milk and continue to beat until well combined.

2 Stir together flour and bicarbonate of soda and stir into butter mixture. Add hazelnuts, chocolate chips, coconut, sultanas and cherries and mix until well combined.

3 Drop tablespoons of mixture onto greased baking trays and bake for 15 minutes or until golden. Remove to wire racks to cool completely.

Makes 25

Glacé fruits such as glacé cherries or pineapple should be rinsed and dried before using in cakes to remove the sugary coating. This helps to prevent the fruit from sinking to the bottom of the cake.

CINNAMON CRISPS

125 g/4 oz butter
1 cup/220 g/7 oz caster sugar
1 egg
1 cup/125 g/4 oz flour
$^{1}/_{2}$ cup/60 g/2 oz self-raising flour
$^{1}/_{2}$ teaspoon bicarbonate of soda
2 teaspoons ground cinnamon

1 Place butter and $^{3}/_{4}$ cup/170 g/5$^{1}/_{2}$ oz sugar in a bowl and beat until light and fluffy. Add egg and beat well.

2 Sift together flour, self-raising flour and bicarbonate of soda and stir into butter mixture. Turn dough onto a floured surface and knead briefly. Wrap in plastic food wrap and refrigerate for 30 minutes or until firm.

3 Place cinnamon and remaining sugar in a small bowl and mix to combine. Roll dough into small balls, then roll balls in sugar mixture and place 5 cm/2 in apart on lightly greased baking trays and bake for 8 minutes or until golden. Remove to wire racks to cool.

Makes 25

Oven temperature
180°C, 350°F, Gas 4

Fat or shortening in whatever form makes a baked product tender and helps to improve its keeping quality. In most baked goods, top quality margarine and butter are interchangeable.

CASHEW NUT COOKIES

Oven temperature
180°C, 350°F, Gas 4

125 g/4 oz butter
$^1/_3$ cup/75 g/2$^1/_2$ oz caster sugar
1 teaspoon vanilla essence
1 egg yolk
1 cup/125 g/4 oz flour, sifted
$^1/_2$ cup/60 g/2 oz self-raising flour, sifted
2 tablespoons wheat germ
60 g/2 oz unsalted cashew nuts, toasted

1 Place butter and sugar in a bowl and beat until light and fluffy. Add vanilla essence and egg yolk and beat to combine.

2 Fold flour, self-raising flour and wheat germ into butter mixture. Turn dough onto a lightly floured surface and knead briefly. Shape into a log, wrap in plastic food wrap and refrigerate for 30 minutes or until firm.

3 Slice dough into 5 mm/$^1/_4$ in slices and place on greased baking trays. Press a cashew nut into the top of each biscuit and bake for 10-12 minutes or until golden.

Makes 48

Toasting nuts increases their flavour. To toast, place on a baking tray and cook at 180°C/350°F/Gas 4 for 5-10 minutes, shaking the tray from time to time. Take care that the nuts do not burn and remove them from the oven as soon as they are golden.

CHOCOLATE ALMOND BALLS

$^1/_2$ cup/125 mL/4 fl oz cream (double)
125 g/4 oz dark chocolate, chopped
15 g/$^1/_2$ oz butter
60 g/2 oz almonds, finely chopped, toasted
30 g/1 oz puffed rice cereal, crushed

1 Place cream and chocolate in a saucepan and cook over a low heat, stirring, until chocolate melts. Remove pan from heat and set aside to cool slightly. Stir in butter, cover and chill.

2 Using an electric mixer, beat chocolate mixture until soft peaks form. Return to the refrigerator until firm.

3 Place almonds and rice cereal in a bowl and mix to combine. Shape teaspoons of chocolate mixture into balls and roll in almond mixture. Store in an airtight container in the refrigerator.

Makes 24

Served with coffee this uncooked biscuit makes a delicious after-dinner treat.

Cashew Nut Cookies,
Chocolate Almond Balls

Muesli Slice

Oven temperature
160°C, 325°F, Gas 3

60 g/2 oz butter
3 tablespoons honey
2 eggs, lightly beaten
1 cup/200 g/6^1/$_2$ oz natural yogurt
250 g/8 oz ricotta cheese
45 g/1^1/$_2$ oz desiccated coconut
45 g/1^1/$_2$ oz flaked almonds
125 g/4 oz raisins, chopped
1 cup/155 g/5 oz wholemeal flour, sifted
and husks returned
3 tablespoons sesame seeds

1 Place butter and honey in a bowl and beat to combine. Gradually mix in eggs and yogurt, then stir in ricotta cheese, coconut, almonds, raisins, flour and sesame seeds.

2 Pour mixture into a greased and lined shallow 18 x 28 cm/7 x 11 in cake tin and bake for 35-40 minutes or until firm and golden brown. Cool slice in tin, then cut into squares.

Makes 24

Date and Seed Bars

Oven temperature
180°C, 350°F, Gas 4

Honey can be used in place of sugar, but you will need to reduce the amount of honey used by one-quarter and bake at a slightly lower temperature. Baked products made with honey brown more quickly than those made with sugar.

90 g/3 oz butter
^{3}/$_4$ cup/185 g/6 oz raw (muscovado)
or demerara sugar
1 egg, lightly beaten
155 g/5 oz dried dates, chopped
1 cup/125 g/4 oz self-raising flour
60 g/2 oz muesli
2 tablespoons sunflower seeds
1 tablespoon poppy seeds
2 tablespoons chopped pumpkin seeds
^{1}/$_2$ cup/100 g/3^1/$_2$ oz natural yogurt

LEMON ICING
15 g/^{1}/$_2$ oz butter
2 tablespoons boiling water
4 tablespoons lemon juice
2 cups/315 g/10 oz icing sugar, sifted

1 Place butter and raw (muscovado) or demerara sugar in a bowl and beat until light and fluffy. Beat in egg, then stir in dates, flour, muesli, sunflower seeds, poppy seeds, pumpkin seeds and yogurt.

2 Spoon mixture into a lightly greased and lined shallow 18 x 28 cm/7 x 11 in cake tin and bake for 25 minutes or until firm and golden. Cool in tin.

3 To make icing, melt butter in hot water, then stir in lemon juice. Add icing sugar and beat until smooth. Spread icing evenly over cold slice. Allow icing to set and cut slice into fingers or squares.

Makes 24

Fruity Rockcakes, Date and Seed Bars,
Oaty Biscuits, Muesli Slice

OATY BISCUITS

Oven temperature
180°C, 350°F, Gas 4

As ovens vary and the type of baking tray you use can affect the cooking of biscuits, always check them for doneness 2-3 minutes before the time indicated in the recipe. Biscuits and cookies are usually cooked when they are a light golden colour.

60 g/2 oz butter
3 tablespoons brown sugar
1 teaspoon vanilla essence
1 egg, lightly beaten
1 cup/90 g/3 oz rolled oats
3 tablespoons wheat germ
$^1/_2$ cup/75 g/2$^1/_2$ oz wholemeal self-raising flour, sifted and husks returned
3 tablespoons chopped pecans
or walnuts
3 tablespoons chopped dried dates

PINK ICING
15 g/$^1/_2$ oz butter
3 tablespoons boiling water
1 cup/155 g/5 oz icing sugar, sifted
few drops red food colouring

1 Place butter in a bowl and beat until light and fluffy. Add brown sugar and vanilla essence and beat to combine. Add egg and beat well.

2 Stir in rolled oats, wheat germ, flour, pecans or walnuts and dates and mix well to combine.

3 Drop teaspoons of mixture onto lightly greased baking trays and bake for 10 minutes or until golden. Remove biscuits from trays and cool on a wire rack.

4 To make icing, melt butter in water. Add icing sugar and beat until smooth. Mix in food colouring to achieve desired colour and place a drop of icing on each biscuit.

Makes 15

FRUITY ROCKCAKES

Oven temperature
180°C, 350°F, Gas 4

Wholemeal flour uses the whole grain so retains all the flavour and nutrients of the grain. Wholemeal flour has a higher bran content than flour, which reduces the effectiveness of the gluten. Therefore, baked goods made with wholemeal flour tend to have a heavier, more dense texture.

2 cups/315 g/10 oz wholemeal self-raising flour, sifted and husks returned
$^1/_2$ teaspoon ground cinnamon
$^1/_3$ cup/90 g/3 oz raw (muscovado)
or demerara sugar
125 g/4 oz butter
125 g/4 oz raisins, chopped
30 g/1 oz dried apples, chopped
1 egg, lightly beaten
$^1/_3$ cup/90 mL/3 fl oz milk

1 Place flour, cinnamon and sugar in a food processor and process to combine. Add butter and process until mixture resembles fine breadcrumbs, then add raisins and apples. With machine running, slowly add egg and milk to form a thick dough.

2 Drop tablespoons of mixture onto greased baking trays and bake for 12-15 minutes, or until cooked through and golden.

Makes 20

CARAMEL SQUARES

SHORTBREAD BASE
100 g/3¹/₂ oz butter
3 tablespoons sugar
60 g/2 oz cornflour, sifted
³/₄ cup/90 g/3 oz flour, sifted

CARAMEL FILLING
125 g/4 oz butter
¹/₂ cup/90 g/3 oz brown sugar
2 tablespoons honey
400 g/12¹/₂ oz canned sweetened
condensed milk
1 teaspoon vanilla essence

CHOCOLATE TOPPING
200 g/6¹/₂ oz dark chocolate, melted

1 To make base, place butter and sugar in a bowl and beat until light and fluffy. Mix in cornflour and flour, turn onto a lightly floured surface and knead briefly, then press into a greased and lined 18 x 28 cm/7 x 11 in shallow cake tin and bake for 25 minutes or until firm.

2 To make filling, place butter, brown sugar and honey in a saucepan and cook over a medium heat, stirring constantly until sugar melts and ingredients are combined. Bring to the boil and simmer for 7 minutes. Beat in condensed milk and vanilla essence, pour filling over base and bake for 20 minutes longer. Set aside to cool completely.

3 Spread melted chocolate over filling, set aside until firm, then cut into squares.

Makes 25

Oven temperature
180°C, 350°F, Gas 4

An electric mixer is an invaluable appliance for the home baker. It makes the beating of whole eggs or egg whites, the beating of egg yolks and sugar and the creaming of butter and sugar effortless tasks. When beating and creaming use a high speed; however, when adding heavier ingredients, reduce the speed so as to avoid damage to your mixer.

Caramel Squares

FRUIT CAKES

*Lighter fruit cakes are popular as everyday cakes
while richer cakes are made for weddings, special anniversaries,
birthdays and, of course, Christmas. Cakes such as the White
Christmas Cake or the Microwave Fruit Cake are also
delicious topped with an icing.*

Dundee Cake

Carrot and Fruit Loaf

Festive Almond Cake

White Christmas Cake

Rich Fruit Cake

Microwave Fruit Cake

Dundee Cake

DUNDEE CAKE

250 g/8 oz butter, softened
1 teaspoon rum essence
1 cup/220 g/7 oz caster sugar
4 eggs, lightly beaten
2 cups/250 g/8 oz flour
1 teaspoon baking powder
3 tablespoons cornflour
250 g/8 oz sultanas
250 g/8 oz currants
125 g/4 oz mixed peel
125 g/4 oz slivered almonds
60 g/2 oz glacé cherries, halved
2 teaspoons finely grated orange rind
1 tablespoon orange juice
45 g/1^1/$_2$ oz blanched almonds

1   Place butter and rum essence in a bowl and beat until light and fluffy. Gradually add sugar, beating well after each addition until mixture is creamy.

2   Add eggs one at a time, beating well after each addition. Sift together flour, baking powder and cornflour and fold into the butter mixture.

3   Stir in sultanas, currants, mixed peel, slivered almonds, cherries, orange rind and orange juice. Spoon mixture into a greased and lined deep 20 cm/8 in cake tin. Decorate top of cake with almonds, arranged in circles, and bake for 2^1/$_2$-3 hours, or until cooked when tested with a skewer. Set aside to cool in tin before turning out.

Makes a 20 cm/8 in round cake

Oven temperature
150°C, 300°F, Gas 2

This traditional Scottish recipe dating right back to the eighteenth century, is characterised by the almonds that decorate the top of the cake.

CARROT AND FRUIT LOAF

2 eggs
1 cup/250 g/8 oz raw (muscavado) or demerara sugar
1 cup/250 mL/8 fl oz vegetable oil
1 cup/155 g/5 oz wholemeal flour
1 cup/125 g/4 oz flour
^{1}/$_2$ teaspoon bicarbonate of soda
1 teaspoon ground mixed spice
155 g/5 oz carrots, grated
60 g/2 oz walnuts, chopped
90 g/3 oz raisins, chopped

1   Place eggs, sugar and oil in a bowl and beat until light and fluffy. Sift together wholemeal flour, flour, bicarbonate of soda and mixed spice and return husks to mixture. Stir flour mixture into egg mixture.

2   Add carrots, walnuts and raisins and mix to combine.

3   Pour batter into a greased and lined 11 x 21 cm/4^1/$_2$ x 8^1/$_2$ in loaf tin and bake for 1^1/$_4$ hours or until cooked when tested with a skewer. Allow to stand for 5 minutes before turning onto wire racks to cool completely.

Makes an 11 x 21 cm/4^1/$_2$ x 8^1/$_2$ in loaf

Oven temperature
180°C, 350°F, Gas 4

Serve this loaf sliced with or without butter, or top with a lemon cream cheese frosting. To make frosting, beat 125 g/4 oz cream cheese until creamy, then beat in 1 teaspoon finely grated lemon rind, 1^1/$_2$ cups/ 250 g/8 oz icing sugar and 2 teaspoons lemon juice.

Right: Festive Almond Cake
Far right: White Christmas Cake

Oven temperature
150°C, 300°F, Gas 2

Dried fruit is usually
prewashed when you
purchase it. However, if you
do need to wash the fruit
before use, drain it well,
spread it on a clean cloth
and dry it in a low oven for
2-3 hours. If the fruit is not
completely dry it will sink to
the bottom of the cake.

FESTIVE ALMOND CAKE

155 g/5 oz glacé apricots, halved
155 g/5 oz red glacé cherries
155 g/5 oz green glacé cherries
90 g/3 oz raisins
125 g/4 oz brazil nuts
100 g/3¹/2 oz pitted prunes
125 g/4 oz pecans or walnuts
100 g/3¹/2 oz ground almonds
¹/2 teaspoon baking powder
3 eggs
2 tablespoons honey
2 teaspoons vanilla essence

1   Place apricots, red cherries, green
cherries, raisins, brazil nuts, prunes,
pecans or walnuts, almonds and baking
powder in a bowl and mix to combine.

2   Place eggs in a bowl and beat until
thick and creamy. Beat in honey and
vanilla essence, then pour egg mixture
into fruit mixture and mix to combine.

3   Divide mixture between two greased
and lined 11 x 21 cm/4¹/2 x 8¹/2 in loaf
tins, pressing down firmly, and bake for
1¹/2 hours. Allow cakes to cool in tins.

*Makes two 11 x 21 cm/4¹/2 x 8¹/2 in
cakes*

WHITE CHRISTMAS CAKE

185 g/6 oz sultanas
220 g/7 oz glacé cherries, halved
1 tablespoon finely grated lemon rind
$^3/_4$ cup/185 mL/6 fl oz brandy
185 g/6 oz butter
$^3/_4$ cup/185 g/6 oz sugar
4 eggs, separated
$2^1/_2$ cups/315 g/10 oz flour
1 teaspoon baking powder
1 teaspoon ground mixed spice
$^1/_2$ teaspoon ground cinnamon
60 g/2 oz blanched almonds

1 Place sultanas, 185 g/6 oz cherries and lemon rind in a bowl, pour over $^1/_2$ cup/125 mL/4 fl oz brandy and mix to combine. Cover and set aside to stand overnight.

2 Place butter in a bowl and beat until light and fluffy. Gradually add sugar, beating well after each addition. Add egg yolks one at a time, beating well after each addition.

3 Sift together flour, baking powder, mixed spice and cinnamon. Fold flour mixture and fruit mixture, alternately, into butter mixture.

4 Place egg whites in a clean bowl and beat until soft peaks form. Fold egg white mixture into fruit mixture. Spoon batter into a greased and lined 20 cm/8 in round cake tin and smooth top with a spatula. Arrange almonds and remaining cherries decoratively on top of cake and bake for $1^1/_2$ hours or until cooked when tested with a skewer. Using skewer, pierce the cake several times then sprinkle with remaining brandy. Wrap cake in a teatowel and set aside to cool completely before turning out.

Makes a 20 cm/8 in round cake

Oven temperature
180°C, 350°F, Gas 4

To prevent dried fruit from sinking to the bottom of a cake, toss the fruit in a tablespoon of the flour used in the recipe before adding to the cake batter.

RICH FRUIT CAKE

Oven temperature
160°C, 325°F, Gas 3

1 kg/2 lb dried mixed fruit
250 g/8 oz dried dates, chopped
125 g/4 oz butter
^{3}/4 cup/125 g/4 oz brown sugar
1 teaspoon ground cinnamon
^{1}/2 cup/125 mL/4 fl oz water
^{1}/2 cup/125 mL/4 fl oz brandy
2 eggs, lightly beaten
1 cup/125 g/4 oz flour
1 cup/125 g/4 oz self-raising flour

To line a loaf tin, cut a strip of baking paper the width of the base of the tin and long enough to come up the shorter sides of the tin and overlap by 2.5 cm/1 in. Grease the tin and line with the paper. When the cake is cooked the unlined sides can be loosened with a knife and the paper ends are used to lift out the cake.

Makes two
11 x 21 cm/4^1/2 x 8^1/2 in cakes

1   Place mixed fruit, dates, butter, sugar, cinnamon and water in a large saucepan and cook over a medium heat, stirring, until butter melts. Bring to the boil, then reduce heat and simmer, uncovered, for 3 minutes. Remove pan from heat and cool to room temperature.

2   Stir brandy and eggs into fruit mixture. Sift together flour and self-raising flour, add to fruit mixture and mix well to combine. Divide batter between two greased and lined 11 x 21 cm/4^1/2 x 8^1/2 in loaf tins and bake for 1^1/4-1^1/2 hours or until cooked when tested with a skewer. Allow to stand in tins for 10 minutes before turning onto a clean teatowel to cool completely.

MICROWAVE FRUIT CAKE

250 g/8 oz sultanas
125 g/4 oz currants
60 g/2 oz mixed peel, chopped
60 g/2 oz glacé cherries, chopped
30 g/1 oz blanched almonds, chopped
1 cup/170 g/5^1/2 oz brown sugar
200 g/6^1/2 oz butter
^{1}/3 cup/90 mL/3 fl oz brandy or sherry
4 eggs
1 cup/125 g/4 oz self-raising flour
^{1}/4 teaspoon ground nutmeg
^{1}/4 teaspoon ground cloves
1 teaspoon ground cinnamon
Parisian essence or gravy browning

The strip of foil should cover only the sides not the base of the dish. The foil prevents the outside of the cake from overcooking and means that you can make a solid cake. This method of cooking cakes in the microwave is not suitable for light cakes or for those with a short cooking time.

Makes a 20 cm/8 in round cake

1   Place sultanas, currants, mixed peel, cherries, almonds, sugar, butter and 2 tablespoons brandy or sherry in a large microwave-safe mixing bowl and cook on HIGH (100%) for 5 minutes. Stir well and set aside to cool.

2   Mix in eggs one at a time, then stir in flour, nutmeg, cloves, cinnamon and enough Parisian essence or gravy browning to give the cake the colour you want. Spoon into a 20 cm/8 in round microwave-safe dish lined with nonstick paper. Place a 5 cm/2 in strip of aluminium foil around the outside of the dish.

3   Cook cake, elevated, on MEDIUM (50%) for 20-25 minutes or until cake is cooked. If cake appears a little moist, remove foil and cook on HIGH (100%) for 3-5 minutes longer. Sprinkle hot cake with remaining brandy or sherry and allow to cool in dish before turning out.

CHOCOLATE

*Chocolate would have to be one of the most popular
ingredients used in baking. A simple buttercake becomes
something special when topped with a chocolate icing or frosting,
and the addition of chocolate chips to a simple biscuit
reminds us of favourite childhood cookies.*

Rich Chocolate Cake

Rich Chocolate Cake

185 g/6 oz butter, softened
1 teaspoon vanilla essence
1¼ cups/280 g/9 oz caster sugar
3 eggs
90 g/3 oz dark chocolate,
melted and cooled
1¾ cups/220 g/7 oz flour
2 teaspoons baking powder
3 tablespoons cocoa powder
¾ cup/185 mL/6 fl oz milk
3 tablespoons strawberry, raspberry
or plum jam

CHOCOLATE BUTTER ICING
125 g/4 oz butter, softened
100 g/3½ oz dark chocolate,
melted and cooled
2 egg yolks
½ cup/75 g/2½ oz icing sugar, sifted

1 Place butter and vanilla essence in a large mixing bowl and beat until light and fluffy. Gradually add caster sugar, beating well after each addition until mixture is creamy. Beat in eggs one at a time, then mix in chocolate.

2 Sift together flour, baking powder and cocoa powder. Fold flour mixture and milk, alternately, into chocolate mixture.

3 Spoon cake batter into a greased and lined deep 20 cm/8 in round cake tin and bake for 50-55 minutes, or until cooked when tested with a skewer. Stand for 5 minutes before turning onto a wire rack to cool completely.

4 To make icing, place butter in a mixing bowl and beat until light and fluffy. Add chocolate, egg yolks and icing sugar and beat until smooth.

5 Split cake in half horizontally and sandwich layers together with jam. Spread icing over top and sides of cake.

Makes a 20 cm/8 in round cake

Oven temperature
180°C, 350°F, Gas 4

To melt chocolate, place it in a heatproof bowl and set aside. Fill a saucepan with enough water to come just under the bowl; the water should not touch the bowl when it is placed in the saucepan. Bring water to the boil, then remove from heat and place chocolate over the hot water. Stand pan off the heat, stirring chocolate occasionally until it melts and is of a smooth consistency. Cool at room temperature.

Jaffa Pecan Cakes

100 g/3½ oz dark chocolate, chopped
125 g/4 oz butter
2 eggs, beaten
2 tablespoons orange-flavoured liqueur
2 teaspoons finely grated orange rind
¾ cup/170 g/5½ oz caster sugar
60 g/2 oz pecan nuts, chopped
½ cup/60 g/2 oz flour, sifted
18 pecan nut halves
30 g/1 oz dark chocolate, melted

1 Place chopped chocolate and butter in a heatproof bowl set over a saucepan of simmering water and cook, stirring, until chocolate and butter melt and mixture is combined. Remove bowl from heat and set aside to cool slightly.

2 Stir eggs, liqueur, orange rind, sugar and chopped pecan nuts into chocolate mixture and mix to combine. Fold in flour.

3 Spoon batter into patty tins lined with paper cake cases, top with a pecan half and bake for 20 minutes or until cakes are cooked when tested with a skewer. Remove cakes from patty tins and allow to cool on wire racks.

4 Drizzle melted chocolate over cakes and set aside to set.

Makes 18 cakes

Oven temperature
180°C, 350°F, Gas 4

You can replace the orange-flavoured liqueur with fresh orange juice in this recipe if you wish.

CHOC-CHIP CHOCOLATE CAKE

Oven temperature
180°C, 350°F, Gas 4

This rich chocolate cake
studded with white
chocolate chips and topped
with a creamy white
chocolate frosting makes the
perfect special occasion
cake.

125 g/4 oz butter, softened
1 cup/220 g/7 oz caster sugar
1 teaspoon vanilla essence
2 eggs
$1^1/_3$ cups/170 g/$5^1/_2$ oz self-raising flour
$^1/_4$ cup/30 g/1 oz cocoa powder
$^1/_2$ teaspoon baking powder
1 cup/250 mL/8 fl oz milk
200 g/$6^1/_2$ oz white chocolate, chopped

WHITE CHOCOLATE FROSTING
125 g/4 oz butter, softened
100 g/$3^1/_2$ oz white chocolate,
melted and cooled
2 egg yolks
$^1/_2$ cup/75 g/$2^1/_2$ oz icing sugar, sifted

1 Place butter, caster sugar and vanilla essence in a bowl and beat until mixture is creamy. Add eggs one at a time, beating well after each addition.

2 Sift together flour, cocoa powder and baking powder. Fold flour mixture and milk, alternately, into butter mixture, then fold in chocolate.

3 Spoon batter into a greased and lined 23 cm/9 in round cake tin and bake for 30-35 minutes or until cooked when tested with a skewer. Stand in tin for 5 minutes before turning onto a wire rack to cool completely.

4 To make frosting, place butter in a bowl and beat until light and fluffy. Add chocolate, egg yolks and icing sugar and beat until smooth. Spread frosting over top and sides of cake.

Makes a 23 cm/9 in round cake

BROWNIES

Oven temperature
180°C, 350°F, Gas 4

Chocolate can be melted
quickly and easily in the
microwave. Place 125 g/4 oz
chocolate in a microwave-
safe glass or ceramic dish
and melt on HIGH (100%) for
1 minute. When melting
chocolate in the microwave
you will find that it tends to
hold its shape, so always stir
it before additional heating.
If the chocolate is not
completely melted, cook for
30 seconds longer, then stir
again.

155 g/5 oz butter, softened
$^1/_2$ cup/170 g/$5^1/_2$ oz honey, warmed
4 teaspoons water
2 eggs, lightly beaten
$1^3/_4$ cups/220 g/7 oz self-raising flour,
sifted
$^2/_3$ cup/100 g/$3^1/_2$ oz brown sugar
125 g/4 oz dark chocolate, melted and
cooled
icing sugar, sifted

1 Place butter, honey, water, eggs, flour, brown sugar and chocolate in a food processor and process until ingredients are combined.

2 Spoon batter into a greased and lined 23 cm/9 in square cake tin and bake for 30-35 minutes or until cooked when tested with a skewer. Stand cake in tin for 5 minutes before turning onto a wire rack to cool completely. Dust with icing sugar and cut into squares.

Makes 25

Chocolate Shortbread, Brownies,
Choc-Chip Chocolate Cake

CHOCOLATE SHORTBREAD

Oven temperature
160°C, 325°F, Gas 3

The secret to crisp, melt-in-the-mouth shortbread is in the kneading. Shortbread should be kneaded with the fingertips only, on a lightly floured surface until the dough is very smooth. Avoid overkneading as this will make the shortbread tough.

250 g/8 oz butter, softened
$^1/_2$ cup/75 g/2$^1/_2$ oz icing sugar
1 cup/125 g/4 oz flour
1 cup/125 g/4 oz cornflour
$^1/_4$ cup/30 g/1 oz cocoa powder

1 Place butter and icing sugar in a bowl and beat until mixture is creamy. Sift together flour, cornflour and cocoa powder. Stir flour mixture into butter mixture.

2 Turn dough onto a lightly floured surface and knead lightly until smooth. Roll teaspoons of mixture into balls, place on greased baking trays, flatten slightly with a fork and bake for 20-25 minutes or until firm. Allow to cool on trays.

Makes 30

CHOCOLATE SIENNA CAKE

Oven temperature
180°C, 350°F, Gas 4

Native to Australia, the macadamia nut has a very hard shell and a delicious rich buttery flavour. In most recipes that call for macadamia nuts, brazil nuts can be used instead.

60 g/2 oz macadamia or brazil nuts, chopped
125 g/4 oz walnuts, chopped
125 g/4 oz almonds, chopped
155 g/5 oz dried dates, chopped
170 g/5$^1/_2$ oz sultanas
30 g/1 oz desiccated coconut
$^1/_2$ cup/60 g/2 oz flour
$^1/_2$ cup/45 g/1$^1/_2$ oz cocoa powder
$^1/_2$ cup/75 g/2$^1/_2$ oz icing sugar
250 g/8 oz milk chocolate, grated
60 g/2 oz butter
$^1/_2$ cup/155 g/5 oz apricot jam

1 Place macadamia or brazil nuts, walnuts, almonds, dates, sultanas, coconut, flour, cocoa powder and icing sugar in a bowl and mix to combine.

2 Place chocolate, butter and apricot jam in a saucepan and cook over a low heat, stirring, until ingredients are melted and combined. Pour chocolate mixture into fruit mixture and mix well.

3 Spoon mixture into a greased and lined shallow 23 cm/9 in round cake tin, pressing down firmly, and bake for 35 minutes.

Makes a 23 cm/9 in round cake

Chocolate Hazelnut Cake

CHOCOLATE HAZELNUT CAKE

30 g/1 oz finely chopped hazelnuts
$^1/_4$ cup/45 g/1$^1/_2$ oz brown sugar
1 packet rich chocolate cake mix

STRAWBERRY SAUCE
250 g/8 oz strawberries
1 tablespoon strawberry jam
1 tablespoon lemon juice

1   Place hazelnuts and sugar in a small bowl and mix to combine. Sprinkle sugar mixture over the base of a greased and lined 11 x 21 cm/4$^1/_2$ x 8$^1/_2$ in loaf tin.

2   Make up packet cake following packet directions. Pour batter into loaf tin and bake according to packet directions.

3   To make sauce, place strawberries, jam and lemon juice in a food processor or blender and process until smooth. Push mixture through a sieve and discard any pips.

4   Allow cake to stand in tin for 5 minutes before turning out. To serve, cut into slices and accompany with sauce.

Serves 8

An easy way to make a packet cake mix into something special. You can use any nuts that you like in place of the hazelnuts. Why not try ground almonds or shredded coconut for something different?

FUDGE CAKE

Oven temperature
180°C, 350°F, Gas 4

Chocolate melts more
rapidly if broken into small
pieces. The container in
which the chocolate is being
melted needs to be
uncovered and completely
dry. Covering can cause
condensation and just one
drop of water will ruin the
chocolate. The melting
process should occur slowly,
as chocolate scorches if
overheated.

90 g/3 oz butter
90 g/3 oz dark chocolate, chopped
4 eggs, separated
1 cup/220 g/7 oz caster sugar
$^1/_4$ cup/60 mL/2 fl oz strong black coffee
60 g/2 oz ground hazelnuts
$^1/_2$ cup/60 g/2 oz flour
$^1/_2$ cup/45 g/1$^1/_2$ oz cocoa powder

PISTACHIO CUSTARD
4 egg yolks, beaten
$^1/_3$ cup/75 g/2$^1/_2$ oz caster sugar
1 cup/250 mL/8 fl oz milk
60 g/2 oz chopped pistachio nuts

1   Place butter and chocolate in a
heatproof bowl set over a saucepan of
simmering water and cook, stirring, until
chocolate and butter melt and mixture is
combined. Remove bowl from heat and
set aside to cool slightly.

2   Place egg yolks and $^2/_3$ cup/140 g/
4$^1/_2$ oz sugar in a bowl and beat until light
and fluffy. Fold coffee, hazelnuts and
chocolate mixture into egg yolk mixture.
Sift together flour and cocoa powder,
then fold into mixture.

3   Place egg whites in a clean bowl and
beat until soft peaks form. Gradually add
remaining sugar, beating well after each
addition until stiff peaks form. Fold egg
white mixture into chocolate mixture.
Spoon into a greased and lined deep
23 cm/9 in flan tin and bake for
30 minutes or until cooked when tested
with a skewer. Stand in tin for 5 minutes
before turning onto a wire rack to cool
completely.

4   To make custard, place egg yolks, sugar
and milk in a heatproof bowl and whisk to
combine. Place bowl over a saucepan of
simmering water and cook, whisking
constantly, until mixture thickens.
Remove from heat, stir in nuts and set
aside to cool. Serve with cake.

Serves 8

Fudge Cake

CHOCOLATE RUM SLICE

Oven temperature
180°C, 350°F, Gas 4

1 cup/125 g/4 oz self-raising flour, sifted
1 tablespoon cocoa powder, sifted
$^1/_2$ cup/100 g/3$^1/_2$ oz caster sugar
75 g/2$^1/_2$ oz desiccated coconut
75 g/2$^1/_2$ oz raisins, chopped
125 g/4 oz butter, melted
1 teaspoon rum essence
2 tablespoons grated dark chocolate

CHOCOLATE FROSTING
1 cup/155 g/5 oz icing sugar
1 tablespoon cocoa powder
15 g/$^1/_2$ oz butter, softened
1 tablespoon boiling water

1 Place flour, cocoa powder, caster sugar, coconut and raisins in a bowl and mix to combine. Stir in butter and rum essence and mix well.

2 Press mixture into a greased and lined 23 cm/9 in square cake tin and bake for 20-25 minutes or until firm. Allow to cool in tin.

3 To make frosting, sift icing sugar and cocoa powder together into a bowl. Add butter and water and beat to make a frosting of a spreadable consistency.

4 Turn slice onto a wire rack or plate, spread with frosting and sprinkle with grated chocolate. Refrigerate until frosting is firm, then cut into squares.

Makes 25

An easy way to grate chocolate is to use the food processor with the shredding disc. With the machine running, place the chocolate in the feed tube and press down firmly on the chocolate.

FRUIT AND NUT BROWNIES

Oven temperature
160°C, 325°F, Gas 3

Two of the easiest chocolate decorations for a baked product are chocolate curls and shavings. Chocolate curls are made from chocolate at room temperature; for shavings the chocolate is chilled first. Using a vegetable peeler, shave the sides of the block of chocolate. Curls or shavings will form depending on the temperature of the chocolate.

125 g/4 oz dark chocolate, chopped
90 g/3 oz butter
2 eggs
1¹/4 cups/280 g/9 oz caster sugar
60 g/2 oz walnuts, chopped
90 g/3 oz chocolate-coated
sultanas or raisins
¹/2 cup/60 g/2 oz self-raising flour, sifted

CHOCOLATE TOPPING
90 g/3 oz dark chocolate, chopped
185 g/6 oz cream cheese
2 tablespoons sugar
1 egg

1 Place chocolate and butter in a heatproof bowl set over a saucepan of simmering water and cook, stirring constantly, until chocolate and butter melt and mixture is combined. Remove bowl from heat and set aside to cool slightly.

2 Place eggs and caster sugar in a bowl and beat until foamy. Fold chocolate mixture, walnuts, sultanas or raisins and flour into egg mixture. Spoon batter into a greased and lined 23 cm/9 in springform tin and bake for 40 minutes or until top is dry but centre is still moist.

3 To make topping, place chocolate in a heatproof bowl set over a saucepan of simmering water and heat until chocolate melts. Remove bowl from heat and set aside to cool slightly. Place cream cheese and sugar in a bowl and beat until smooth. Beat in egg, then chocolate mixture and continue beating until well combined. Pour topping over hot brownies and bake for 15 minutes longer. Allow to cool in tin, then refrigerate for 2 hours before cutting into wedges and serving.

Serves 10

DEVIL'S FOOD CAKE

CHOCOLATE

1 cup/100 g/3¹/₂ oz cocoa powder
1¹/₂ cups/375 mL/12 fl oz boiling water
375 g/12 oz unsalted butter, softened
1 teaspoon vanilla essence
1¹/₂ cups/330 g/10¹/₂ oz caster sugar
4 eggs
2¹/₂ cups/315 g/10 oz flour
¹/₂ cup/60 g/2 oz cornflour
1 teaspoon bicarbonate of soda
1 teaspoon salt
¹/₂ cup/125 mL/4 fl oz cream (double), whipped

CHOCOLATE BUTTER ICING
250 g/8 oz butter, softened
1 egg
2 egg yolks
1 cup/155 g/5 oz icing sugar, sifted
185 g/6 oz dark chocolate, melted and cooled

1 Place cocoa powder and water in a bowl and mix until blended. Set aside to cool. Place butter and vanilla essence in a bowl and beat until light and fluffy. Gradually add caster sugar, beating well after each addition until mixture is creamy. Beat in eggs one at a time, beating well after each addition.

2 Sift together flour, cornflour, bicarbonate of soda and salt. Fold flour mixture and cocoa mixture, alternately, into egg mixture.

3 Divide batter between three greased and lined 23 cm/9 in sandwich tins and bake for 20-25 minutes or until cakes are cooked when tested with a skewer. Stand in tins for 5 minutes before turning onto wire racks to cool completely.

4 To make icing, place butter in a bowl and beat until light and fluffy. Mix in egg, egg yolks and icing sugar. Add chocolate and beat until icing is thick and creamy. Sandwich cakes together using whipped cream, then cover top and sides with icing.

Makes a 23 cm/9 in round cake

Oven temperature
180°C, 350°F, Gas 4

Chocolate 'seizes' if it is overheated or if it comes in contact with water or steam. Seizing results in the chocolate tightening and becoming a thick mass that will not melt. To rescue seized chocolate, stir a little cream or vegetable oil into the chocolate until it becomes smooth again.

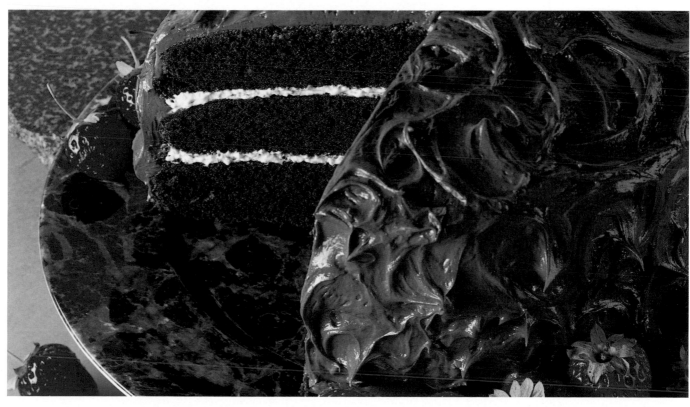

41

CAKES

Don't just save these cakes for a special occasion.
Your family and friends will be delighted when you open a
cake tin that actually contains a homemade cake. Most of the
cakes in this chapter will keep in an airtight container for 3-5
days or can be frozen for longer keeping.

Crumble Berry Cake

CRUMBLE BERRY CAKE

BERRY CAKE
60 g/2 oz butter
$^3/4$ cup/170 g/5$^1/2$ oz caster sugar
1 egg
1 cup/125 g/4 oz flour
1 cup/125 g/4 oz self-raising flour
$^1/2$ cup/125 mL/4 fl oz milk
250 g/8 oz fresh or frozen blackberries
or raspberries

CRUMBLE TOPPING
60 g/2 oz butter
$^1/2$ cup/90 g/3 oz brown sugar
$^1/2$ cup/60 g/2 oz flour
$^1/2$ teaspoon ground mixed spice

BERRY SAUCE
250 g/8 oz fresh or frozen blackberries
or raspberries
3 tablespoons caster sugar
2 tablespoons lemon juice

1   To make topping, place butter, brown sugar, flour and mixed spice in a food processor and process until mixture resembles fine breadcrumbs. Set aside.

2   To make cake, place butter and caster sugar in a bowl and beat until light and fluffy. Beat in egg. Sift together flour and self-raising flour. Fold flour mixture and milk, alternately, into butter mixture, then stir in berries.

3   Spoon batter into a greased and lined 20 cm/8 in springform tin. Sprinkle cake with topping and bake for 45 minutes or until cooked when tested with a skewer. Allow cake to cool in tin for 10 minutes before removing to a wire rack to cool completely.

4   To make sauce, place berries, sugar and lemon juice in a food processor or blender and process until smooth. Push sauce through a sieve and discard pips. Serve sauce with cake.

Makes a 20 cm/8 in round cake

Oven temperature
180°C, 350°F, Gas 4

To test if your cake is cooked, insert a skewer into the thickest part of the cake. If the skewer comes away clean, your cake is cooked. If there is still cake mixture on the skewer, cook cake for 5 minutes longer then test again.

'When baking a cake, do not open the oven door until at least halfway through the recommended cooking time or the rising process will be interrupted. The sudden drop in temperature will cause the cake to sink.'

SPICED APPLE CAKE

Oven temperature
180°C, 350°F, Gas 4

The best way to cut a delicate cake is to use a long sharp knife. Dip the knife into a jug of hot water, then shake off the water and cut your cake. The blade of the hot knife will melt through the icing and filling and so make a clean cut in the cake that does not tear the delicate structure. Wipe the blade of the knife with a damp cloth before cutting the next slice of cake. Dip the knife in the hot water again as the blade becomes cool.

2 apples, cored, peeled and sliced
$^3/_4$ cup/185 mL/6 fl oz water
125 g/4 oz butter
1 cup/250 g/8 oz raw (muscovado) or demerara sugar
2 eggs
1 cup/125 g/4 oz self-raising flour
1 cup/155 g/5 oz wholemeal flour
$^1/_2$ teaspoon bicarbonate of soda
1 teaspoon ground mixed spice
30 g/1 oz walnuts, chopped
60 g/2 oz raisins, chopped
$^3/_4$ cup/185 mL/6 fl oz cream (double), whipped
icing sugar, sifted

1   Place apples and water in a saucepan and cook over a medium heat until tender. Place in a food processor or blender and process until smooth. Set aside to cool.

2   Place butter and sugar in a bowl and beat until light and fluffy. Add eggs one at a time, beating well after each addition.

3   Sift together self-raising flour, wholemeal flour, bicarbonate of soda and mixed spice into a bowl. Return husks to bowl. Mix flour mixture and apple mixture, alternately, into butter mixture, then stir in walnuts and raisins.

4   Spoon batter into a greased and lined 23 cm/9 in round cake tin and bake for 40 minutes or until cooked when tested with a skewer. Allow to cool in tin for 5 minutes before turning onto a wire rack to cool completely.

5   Split cake in half horizontally, spread bottom half with cream then top with other half and dust with icing sugar.

Makes a 23 cm/9 in round cake

Left: Spiced Apple Cake
Below: Orange Poppy Seed Cake, Madeira Cake

ORANGE POPPY SEED CAKE

4 tablespoons poppy seeds
$^1/_4$ cup/60 mL/2 fl oz orange juice
125 g/4 oz natural yogurt
185 g/6 oz butter, softened
1 tablespoon finely grated orange rind
1 cup/220 g/7 oz caster sugar
3 eggs
2 cups/250 g/8 oz self-raising flour,
sifted

Makes a 20 cm/8 in ring cake

1 Place poppy seeds, orange juice and yogurt in a bowl, mix to combine, and set aside to stand for 1 hour.

2 Place butter and orange rind in a bowl and beat until light and fluffy. Gradually add sugar, beating well after each addition until mixture is creamy.

3 Add eggs one at a time, beating well after each addition. Fold flour and poppy seed mixture, alternately, into butter mixture.

4 Spoon batter into a greased 20 cm/8 in fluted ring tin and bake for 35-40 minutes or until cooked when tested with a skewer. Stand in tin for 5 minutes before turning onto a wire rack to cool completely.

Oven temperature
180°C, 350°F, Gas 4

You will find that a freshly baked cake is fragile. Allow the cake to cool for a short time in the tin before turning onto a wire rack to cool completely.

45

MADEIRA CAKE

In the nineteenth century a glass of Madeira with a slice of Madeira cake was often served to morning callers. For the best flavour, use butter when making Madeira Cake.

250 g/8 oz butter, softened
2 teaspoons vanilla essence
1 teaspoon finely grated lemon rind
2 cups/440 g/14 oz caster sugar
6 eggs
1^1/$_2$ cups/185 g/6 oz flour
1 cup/125 g/4 oz self-raising flour
250 g/8 oz natural yogurt

LEMON ICING
1^1/$_2$ cups/250 g/8 oz icing sugar, sifted
1 tablespoon lemon juice
30 g/1 oz butter, softened
2 tablespoons shredded coconut, toasted

1   Place butter, vanilla essence and lemon rind in a bowl and beat until light and fluffy. Gradually add caster sugar, beating well after each addition until mixture is creamy.

2   Add eggs one at a time, beating well after each addition. Sift together flour and self-raising flour. Fold flour mixture and yogurt, alternately, into butter mixture. Spoon batter into a greased and lined 23 cm/9 in square cake tin and bake for 1 hour or until cake is cooked when tested with a skewer. Stand in tin for 10 minutes before turning onto a wire rack to cool completely.

3   To make icing, place icing sugar, lemon juice and butter in a bowl and mix until smooth. Add a little more lemon juice if necessary. Spread icing over cake and sprinkle with coconut.

Makes a 23 cm/9 in square cake

FRUIT SHORTCAKE

Most undecorated cakes can be frozen successfully. Wrap the cake in freezer wrap or place in a freezer bag and seal. To thaw a frozen cake, leave in package and thaw at room temperature. Large cakes will take 3-4 hours to thaw, layer cakes 1-2 hours and small cakes about 30 minutes.

2 cups/250 g/8 oz self-raising flour, sifted
125 g/4 oz butter
^{1}/$_2$ cup/100 g/3^1/$_2$ oz caster sugar, plus 2 tablespoons
1 egg, beaten
1 tablespoon lemon juice
200 g/6^1/$_2$ oz prepared mincemeat
1 egg white, lightly beaten

1   Place flour, butter and ^{1}/$_2$ cup/100 g/3^1/$_2$ oz sugar in a food processor and process until mixture resembles fine breadcrumbs. With machine running, slowly add egg and enough lemon juice to make a firm dough. Turn onto a floured surface and knead briefly. Wrap dough in plastic food wrap and refrigerate for 30 minutes.

2   Divide dough in half. Roll out one half large enough to cover the base and sides of a greased 20 cm/8 in sandwich tin. Spread mincemeat over base.

3   Roll out remaining dough large enough to cover mincemeat. Press edges together firmly. Brush with egg white and sprinkle with remaining sugar. Bake for 30-35 minutes or until cooked. Stand for 10 minutes before turning onto a wire rack to cool completely.

Serves 8

APRICOT UPSIDE-DOWN CAKE

60 g/2 oz dried apricots
60 g/2 oz butter, softened
$^1/_2$ cup/90 g/3 oz brown sugar
4 tablespoons chopped walnuts

GINGERBREAD
1 cup/125 g/4 oz flour
$^1/_2$ cup/60 g/2 oz self-raising flour
$^1/_2$ teaspoon bicarbonate of soda
3 teaspoons ground ginger
$^1/_2$ teaspoon ground nutmeg
$^1/_2$ cup/90 g/3 oz brown sugar
$^1/_2$ cup/170 g/5$^1/_2$ oz golden syrup
$^1/_2$ cup/125 mL/4 fl oz water
125 g/4 oz butter

1 Place apricots in a bowl, pour over enough boiling water to cover and set aside to soak for 30 minutes. Drain and set aside.

2 Place butter and sugar in a bowl and beat until light and fluffy. Spread butter mixture over the base of a greased and lined 20 cm/8 in ring tin. Sprinkle with walnuts and top with apricots, cut side up.

3 To make Gingerbread, sift together flour, self-raising flour, bicarbonate of soda, ginger and nutmeg into a bowl. Add sugar and mix to combine. Place golden syrup, water and butter in a saucepan and cook over a low heat, stirring, until butter is melted and ingredients are combined. Remove pan from heat and set aside to cool slightly.

4 Stir golden syrup mixture into dry ingredients and mix well to combine. Spoon batter into prepared cake tin and bake for 35-40 minutes or until cooked when tested with a skewer. Allow to stand in tin for 15 minutes before turning onto a wire rack to cool completely.

Makes a 20 cm/8 in ring cake

Oven temperature
180°C, 350°F, Gas 4

Keeping times for cakes vary, depending on the ingredients used. A fatless sponge will stay fresh for 1-2 days only while one made with fat will keep fresh for 3 days. Cakes made using the creaming method usually keep fresh for up to a week. Light fruit cakes keep for 2-3 weeks and heavy rich fruit cakes will store for a month or more.

Apricot Upside-down Cake, Fruit Shortcake

QUICK BREADS

*Quick breads, true to their name, are quick – and easy –
to bake. They use baking powder or bicarbonate of soda instead
of yeast as the rising agent. In this chapter you will find recipes
for such delicious quick breads as Bacon Corn Bread Pots, Herb
Rolls, and Carrot and Sesame Muffins.*

Scones

SCONES

2 cups/250 g/8 oz self-raising flour
1 teaspoon baking powder
2 teaspoons sugar
45 g/1^1/$_2$ oz butter
1 egg
^{1}/$_2$ cup/125 mL/4 fl oz milk

1 Sift together flour and baking powder into a large bowl. Stir in sugar, then rub in butter, using fingertips, until mixture resembles coarse breadcrumbs.

2 Whisk together egg and milk. Make a well in centre of flour mixture, pour in egg mixture and mix to form a soft dough. Turn onto a lightly floured surface and knead lightly.

3 Press dough out to a 2 cm/^{3}/$_4$ in thickness, using palm of hand. Cut out scones using a floured 5 cm/2 in cutter. Avoid twisting the cutter, or the scones will rise unevenly.

4 Arrange scones close together on a greased and lightly floured baking tray or in a shallow 20 cm/8 in round cake tin. Brush with a little milk and bake for 12-15 minutes or until golden.

Makes 12

Oven temperature
220°C, 425°F, Gas 7

To grease and flour a cake tin or baking tray, lightly brush with melted butter or margarine, then sprinkle with flour and shake to coat evenly. Invert on work surface and tap gently to remove excess flour.

SODA BREAD

4 cups/500 g/1 lb flour
1 teaspoon bicarbonate of soda
1 teaspoon salt
45 g/1^1/$_2$ oz butter
2 cups/500 mL/16 fl oz buttermilk
or milk

1 Sift together flour, bicarbonate of soda and salt into a bowl. Rub in butter, using fingertips, until mixture resembles coarse breadcrumbs. Make a well in the centre of the flour mixture and pour in milk. Using a round-ended knife, mix to form a soft dough.

2 Turn dough onto a floured surface and knead lightly until smooth. Shape into an 18 cm/7 in round and place on a greased and floured baking tray. Score dough into eighths using a sharp knife. Dust lightly with flour and bake for 35-40 minutes or until loaf sounds hollow when tapped on the base.

Serves 8

Oven temperature
200°C, 400°F, Gas 6

A loaf for when you need bread unexpectedly, Soda Bread is made with bicarbonate of soda rather than yeast so requires no rising. It is best eaten slightly warm and is delicious with lashings of treacle or golden syrup.

CHILLI SOUP BISCUITS

Oven temperature
220°C, 425°F, Gas 7

2 rashers bacon, finely chopped
2 cups/250 g/8 oz flour
3 teaspoons baking powder
$^1/_2$ teaspoon salt
90 g/3 oz butter
90 g/3 oz grated tasty cheese
(mature Cheddar)
2 small fresh red chillies, seeded and
finely chopped
$^2/_3$ cup/170 mL/5$^1/_2$ fl oz milk
30 g/1 oz butter, melted

1 Cook bacon in a nonstick frying pan over a medium high heat for 3-4 minutes or until crisp. Remove from pan and drain on absorbent kitchen paper.

2 Sift together flour, baking powder and salt into a bowl. Rub in butter with fingertips until mixture resembles coarse breadcrumbs.

3 Stir bacon, cheese and chillies into flour mixture. Add milk and mix to form a soft dough. Turn onto a lightly floured surface and knead lightly with fingertips until smooth.

4 Using heel of hand, gently press dough out to 1 cm/$^1/_2$ in thick. Cut out rounds using a 5 cm/2 in pastry cutter. Place on a greased baking tray and brush with melted butter. Bake for 12-15 minutes or until golden brown. Remove from tray and cool on a wire rack or serve warm spread with butter.

Makes 16

HERB ROLLS

Oven temperature
180°C, 350°F, Gas 4

90 g/3 oz butter
8 spring onions, finely chopped
2$^1/_2$ cups/315 g/10 oz flour
1 cup/125 g/4 oz self-raising flour
3 teaspoons baking powder
$^1/_2$ teaspoon bicarbonate of soda
4 teaspoons sugar
1 tablespoon finely chopped
fresh parsley
1 tablespoon finely chopped fresh basil
$^1/_2$ cup/125 mL/4 fl oz buttermilk
or milk
3 eggs, lightly beaten
1 egg, beaten with 1$^1/_2$ tablespoons
olive oil

Spring onions and herbs have been added to this soda bread recipe. The dough is then formed into rolls to make the quickest herb-flavoured rolls ever.

1 Melt butter in a frying pan and cook spring onions over a medium heat for 2-3 minutes or until soft. Remove from heat and set aside.

2 Sift together flour and self-raising flour, baking powder and bicarbonate of soda into a large bowl. Stir in sugar, parsley and basil. Combine milk, eggs and onion mixture and mix into flour mixture to form a firm dough.

3 Turn onto a floured surface and knead lightly until smooth. Divide dough into twelve equal portions, roll each portion into a ball and place on greased and floured baking trays. Brush each roll with egg and oil mixture and bake for 30-35 minutes or until golden and cooked through.

Makes 12

Herb Rolls, Soda Bread, Chilli Soup Biscuits

HERB AND CHEESE LOAF

Oven temperature
180°C, 350°F, Gas 4

1¼ cups/185 g/6 oz self-raising
wholemeal flour
1 cup/90 g/3 oz rolled oats
45 g/1½ oz unprocessed bran
60 g/2 oz grated tasty cheese
(mature Cheddar)
1 tablespoon grated Parmesan cheese
2 tablespoons snipped fresh chives
2 tablespoons chopped fresh parsley
1 cup/250 mL/8 fl oz milk
⅓ cup/90 mL/3 fl oz vegetable oil
3 egg whites

1 Place flour, rolled oats, bran, tasty cheese (mature Cheddar), Parmesan cheese, chives and parsley in a bowl and mix to combine. Make a well in the centre of the flour mixture, add milk and oil and mix well to combine.

2 Place egg whites in a clean bowl and beat until stiff peaks form. Fold egg whites into batter.

3 Spoon batter into a greased and lined 11 x 21 cm/4½ x 8½ in loaf tin and bake for 40 minutes or until cooked when tested with a skewer.

Makes an 11 x 21 cm/4½ x 8½ in loaf

This high-fibre loaf is terrific served warm.

CARROT AND SESAME MUFFINS

Oven temperature
200°C, 400°F, Gas 6

3 cups/375 g/12 oz self-raising flour
½ teaspoon bicarbonate of soda
1 teaspoon ground mixed spice
½ cup/90 g/3 oz brown sugar
1 large carrot, grated
4 tablespoons toasted sesame seeds
170 g/5½ oz sultanas
1 cup/200 g/6½ oz natural yogurt
1 cup/250 mL/8 fl oz milk
3 tablespoons melted butter
3 egg whites, lightly beaten

1 Sift together flour, bicarbonate of soda and mixed spice into a large bowl. Add sugar, carrot, sesame seeds and sultanas and mix to combine.

2 Place yogurt, milk, butter and egg whites in a bowl and whisk to combine. Stir yogurt mixture into flour mixture and mix until just combined. Spoon batter into lightly greased muffin tins and bake for 20 minutes or until golden and cooked.

Makes 24

Delicious light muffins are perfect weekend fare. Any leftovers can be frozen and used when time is short.

*Herb and Cheese Loaf,
Carrot and Sesame Muffins*

BACON CORN BREAD POTS

4 rashers bacon, finely chopped
1½ cups/250 g/8 oz fine corn meal
(polenta)
1 cup/125 g/4 oz flour
2½ teaspoons baking powder
4 teaspoons sugar
½ teaspoon salt
60 g/2 oz grated Parmesan cheese
90 g/3 oz butter, chopped
2 eggs, lightly beaten
1¼ cups/315 mL/10 fl oz buttermilk
or milk

Oven temperature
200°C, 400°F, Gas 6

1 Cook bacon in a nonstick frying pan over a medium heat for 3-4 minutes or until crisp. Remove bacon from pan and drain on absorbent kitchen paper.

2 Place corn meal (polenta), flour, baking powder, sugar, salt, Parmesan cheese and butter in a food processor and process until mixture resembles fine breadcrumbs.

3 Combine eggs and milk and, with machine running, pour into corn meal (polenta) mixture and process until combined and batter is smooth. Take care not to overmix. Stir in bacon.

4 Spoon batter into three medium-sized terracotta flowerpots lined with well-greased aluminium foil. Place on a baking tray and bake for 25-30 minutes or until golden.

Serves 6
Makes 3 medium-sized flowerpot loaves

Cooked in flowerpots these tasty corn bread loaves are a perfect accompaniment to soup or salad. Remember that the size of the flowerpots you use will determine the number of loaves you produce.

*From left: Basic Butter Cake,
Apple Cake, Coffee Cake*

BASICS

*In this chapter you will find a butter cake recipe and
a biscuit recipe that can be made into whatever flavours or
shapes that you like. These recipes make great everyday
cakes and biscuits and are ideal for a cake stall.*

BASIC BUTTER CAKE

125 g/4 oz butter
1 teaspoon vanilla essence
$^3/_4$ cup/170 g/5$^1/_2$ oz caster sugar
2 eggs
1$^1/_2$ cups/185 g/6 oz flour, sifted
1$^1/_2$ teaspoons baking powder
$^1/_2$ cup/125 mL/4 fl oz milk

1 Place butter and vanilla essence in a bowl and beat until light and fluffy. Gradually add sugar, beating well after each addition.

2 Add eggs one at a time, beating well after each addition. Sift together flour and baking powder. Fold flour mixture and milk, alternately, into butter mixture.

3 Spoon batter into prepared cake tin and bake according to size of tin you have chosen (see Cake Cooking Chart). Allow cake to stand in tin for 5 minutes before turning onto a wire rack to cool completely. When cold, top with a frosting or icing of your choice.

Before turning out a cake, loosen the sides with a spatula or palette knife. Then turn the cake onto a wire rack and immediately invert onto a second wire rack to cool, so that the top of the cake is not marked with indentations from the rack. If you do not have a second wire rack, invert the cake first onto a clean cloth on your hand then turn it back onto the wire rack.

BUTTER CAKE VARIATIONS

Chocolate Cake: Mix 60 g/2 oz melted chocolate into the basic cake mixture before adding flour mixture and milk. Replace 2 tablespoons flour with 2 tablespoons cocoa powder. Bake according to tin size you have chosen.

Apple Cake: Spread two-thirds of the cake mixture into a prepared cake tin. Top with 200 g/6^1/$_2$ oz cold stewed apple, then remaining cake mixture. Bake according to tin size you have chosen. Allow to stand for 10 minutes before turning onto a wire rack to cool completely.

Orange Cake: Replace vanilla essence with 2 teaspoons finely grated orange rind when beating butter. Replace ^{1}/$_3$ cup/ 90 mL/3 fl oz milk with ^{1}/$_3$ cup/ 90 mL/3 fl oz orange juice. Bake according to tin size you have chosen.

Coffee Cake: Replace vanilla essence with 1 tablespoon instant coffee powder dissolved in 1 tablespoon boiling water. Cool, then add to butter when beating. Bake according to tin size you have chosen.

Coconut Cake: Replace vanilla essence with ^{1}/$_2$ teaspoon coconut essence (optional) and add 45 g/1^1/$_2$ oz desiccated coconut to flour mixture. Bake according to tin size you have chosen.

Banana Cake: Omit milk from recipe. Add 3 small ripe mashed bananas to the butter and egg mixture. Sift together flour, baking powder and 1 teaspoon bicarbonate of soda and fold into banana mixture. Bake according to tin size you have chosen.

Cook cakes in the centre of the oven. You can cook more than one cake at a time. Place them on the same shelf, making sure that the tins do not touch each other, the sides or back of the oven, or the oven door when closed. Reverse positions of cake tins halfway through cooking.

CAKE COOKING CHART

Tin Size	Type	Mixture Quantity	Oven Temp °C	Oven Temp °F	Cooking Time (mins)
18 cm/7 in	round	1	180	350	40-45
20 cm/8 in	round	1	180	350	45
23 cm/9 in	round	1^1/$_2$	180	350	50-55
18 cm/7 in	square	1	180	350	45-50
20 cm 8 in	square	1	180	350	40-45
23 cm/9 in	square	2	180	350	50-55
23 cm/9 in	ring	1	180	350	35-40
18 cm x 28 cm/ 7 in x 11^1/$_4$ in	slab	1	180	350	30-35
11 cm x 21 cm/ 4^1/$_2$ x 8^1/$_2$ in	loaf	1	180	350	60

CHOCOLATE RIPPLE CREAM

100 g/3¹/₂ oz dark chocolate
1 cup/250 mL/8 fl oz cream (double),
well chilled and whipped

Melt chocolate in a small bowl set over a saucepan of simmering water, or melt in the microwave on HIGH (100%) for 45-60 seconds. Fold melted chocolate into chilled cream.

Enough to fill and top a 20 cm/8 in cake

The secret to making Chocolate Ripple Cream is to have the cream well chilled before folding the chocolate through. It makes a wonderful topping or filling for a chocolate cake or sponge.

BUTTERSCOTCH FROSTING

1¹/₂ cups/250 g/8 oz brown sugar
¹/₄ cup/60 mL/2 fl oz milk
30 g/1 oz butter
1 cup/155 g/5 oz icing sugar

Place sugar, milk and butter in a saucepan and cook over a low heat, stirring constantly, until sugar dissolves. Bring to the boil and boil for 3-4 minutes. Remove from heat and set aside to cool until just warm, then beat in icing sugar until frosting is of a spreadable consistency. Use immediately.

Enough to cover a 20 cm/8 in cake

MOCK CREAM

60 g/2 oz butter
¹/₄ cup/60 g/2 oz caster sugar
¹/₄ cup/60 mL/2 fl oz boiling water
¹/₄ teaspoon vanilla essence

Place butter and sugar in a bowl and add boiling water. Beat, using an electric mixer, until creamy. Beat in vanilla essence.

Enough to fill a 20 cm/8 in cake

If the mixture curdles, place over a saucepan of simmering water and continue beating.

VANILLA BUTTER ICING

Chocolate Butter Icing: Add
1/4 cup/30 g/1 oz cocoa
powder to boiling water.
Coffee Butter Icing: Add 1
tablespoon instant coffee
powder to boiling water.
Lemon Butter Icing: Replace
vanilla essence with 1-2
teaspoons lemon juice.
Passion Fruit Icing: Replace
vanilla essence with 2-3
tablespoons passion fruit
pulp. A little more icing sugar
may be required to make an
icing of spreadable
consistency.

1 1/2 cups/250 g/8 oz icing sugar, sifted
60 g/2 oz butter
2 tablespoons boiling water
1/4 teaspoon vanilla essence
few drops of food colouring (optional)

Place icing sugar and butter in a bowl, add boiling water and mix to make an icing of spreadable consistency, adding a little more water if necessary. Beat in vanilla essence and food colouring, if using.

Enough to cover a 20 cm/8 in cake or 18 biscuits

MARSHMALLOW FROSTING

1 egg white
2 teaspoons gelatine dissolved in
1/2 cup/125 mL/4 fl oz hot water, cooled
1 cup/155 g/5 oz icing sugar
flavouring of your choice
few drops of food colouring (optional)

Place egg white in a bowl and beat until soft peaks form, then continue beating while gradually adding gelatine mixture. Beat in icing sugar, flavouring and colouring, if using. Continue beating until frosting is thick.

Enough to fill and cover a 20 cm/8 in cake

CHOCOLATE FUDGE ICING

$^3/_4$ cup/170 g/5$^1/_2$ oz caster sugar
$^1/_3$ cup/90 mL/3 fl oz evaporated milk
125 g/4 oz dark chocolate, broken
into pieces
45 g/1$^1/_2$ oz butter
$^1/_4$ teaspoon vanilla essence

1 Place sugar and evaporated milk in a
heavy-based saucepan and cook over a
low heat, stirring, until sugar dissolves.
Bring mixture to the boil and simmer,
stirring constantly, for 4 minutes.

2 Remove pan from heat and stir in
chocolate. Continue stirring until
chocolate melts, then stir in butter and
vanilla essence.

3 Transfer frosting to a bowl and set
aside to cool. Cover with plastic food
wrap and chill until frosting thickens and
is of a spreadable consistency.

*Enough to fill and cover a 20 cm/8 in
cake*

BASIC BISCUITS

Oven temperature
180°C, 350°F, Gas 4

125 g/4 oz butter
^{3}/4 cup/170 g/5^1/2 oz caster sugar
1 teaspoon vanilla essence
1 egg
1 cup/125 g/4 oz flour, sifted
1 cup/125 g/4 oz self-raising flour, sifted

1   Place butter, sugar and vanilla essence in a bowl and beat until light and fluffy. Add egg and beat well. Fold in flour and self-raising flour, cover and refrigerate for 2 hours.

2   Roll heaped teaspoons of mixture into balls. Place on greased baking trays, spacing well apart to allow for spreading. Flatten each biscuit slightly with a fork and bake for 12-15 minutes or until golden. Allow to cool on trays for a few minutes before transferring to wire racks to cool completely.

Makes 40

VARIATIONS

Spicy Fruit Cookies: Replace ^{1}/3 cup/ 75 g/2^1/2 oz caster sugar with ^{1}/3 cup/60 g/ 2 oz brown sugar. Sift 2 teaspoons ground cinnamon, 1 teaspoon ground mixed spice and 1 teaspoon ground ginger with flour. Roll out mixture and cut out 32 rounds with a 5 cm/2 in biscuit cutter. Top half the rounds with a teaspoon of mincemeat and cover with remaining rounds. Press edges lightly to seal and bake for 20-25 minutes or until golden.

Three-Chocolate Cookies: Add 45 g/ 1^1/2 oz finely chopped dark chocolate, 45 g/1^1/2 oz finely chopped milk chocolate and 45 g/1^1/2 oz finely chopped white chocolate to biscuit mixture after beating in egg. Drop teaspoons of mixture onto greased baking trays and bake for 12-15 minutes or until golden.

Creamy Jam Drops: Roll heaped teaspoons of mixture into balls, place on lightly greased baking trays and flatten slightly. Make indents in the centre of each round and fill with a small amount of cream cheese and top with a teaspoon of jam of your choice. Be careful not to fill the holes too much, or the jam will overflow during cooking. Bake for 12-15 minutes or until golden.

Date Wraps: Place 20 dried dates in a small bowl, pour over 4 tablespoons brandy and set aside to soak for 30 minutes. Drain and set aside. Divide biscuit dough into 20 equal portions. Mould each portion around a date. Place on greased baking trays and bake at 160°C/325°F/Gas 3 for 20-25 minutes or until golden.

When baking, make sure your butter and eggs are at room temperature before you start, unless the recipe states otherwise.

Basic Biscuits, Spicy Fruit Cookies,
Three-Chocolate Cookies, Creamy Jam Drops,
Date Wraps

DANISH PASTRIES

Serve these easy Danish Pastries for breakfast or brunch, with morning coffee or afternoon tea. No matter what the occasion, they are sure to impress.

Oven temperature
220°C, 425°F, Gas 7

FOR EACH FILLING YOU WILL NEED
300 g/9^1/$_2$ oz prepared puff pastry
^{1}/$_2$ cup/155 g/5 oz apricot jam
1 tablespoon water

APRICOT FILLING
8 canned apricot halves, drained

CREAM CHEESE FILLING
200 g/6^1/$_2$ oz cream cheese
1 egg yolk
2 tablespoons caster sugar

CHERRY FILLING
750 g/1^1/$_2$ lb bottled, pitted morello cherries, drained
^{1}/$_4$ cup/60 g/2 oz caster sugar
1 teaspoon ground cinnamon

1 Roll out pastry to 3 mm/^{1}/$_8$ in thick.

2 To make Apricot Danish Pastries, cut pastry into eight 10 cm/4 in squares. Make four 5 cm/2 in cuts, starting from each corner and cutting towards the centre of each pastry square. Fold one half of each corner to centre and place an apricot over the top.

3 To make Sweet Cheese Pastries, place cream cheese, egg yolk and sugar in a food processor or blender and process until smooth. Cut pastry into eight 12 cm/4^3/$_4$ in squares. Spread filling over half of each pastry square leaving a 1 cm/^{1}/$_2$ in border. Brush edge with a little water and fold pastry over to enclose filling. Press edges firmly together to seal. Cut six 3 cm/1^1/$_4$ in slits along joined edges of pastry.

4 To make Cherry Squares, combine cherries, sugar and cinnamon in a bowl. Cut pastry into eight 12 cm/4^3/$_4$ in squares. Roll in edges to form a narrow rim, then place a spoonful of cherry mixture in centre of each pastry square.

5 Place prepared pastries on greased oven trays and bake for 15-20 minutes or until golden.

6 To make glaze, place jam and water in a saucepan and cook over a high heat until mixture boils. Remove from heat and brush over hot pastries.

Makes 8 of each pastry

Sweet Cheese Pastry, Apricot Danish Pastry,
Cherry Squares

COCONUT ANGEL FOOD CAKE

$^3/_4$ cup/90 g/3 oz flour
$^1/_4$ cup/30 g/1 oz cornflour
1 cup/220 g/7 oz caster sugar
10 egg whites
$^1/_2$ teaspoon salt
1 teaspoon cream of tartar
8 teaspoons water
1 teaspoon vanilla essence
45 g/1$^1/_2$ oz shredded coconut

FLUFFY FROSTING
$^1/_2$ cup/125 mL/4 fl oz water
1$^1/_4$ cups/315 g/10 oz sugar
3 egg whites
90 g/3 oz shredded coconut, lightly
toasted

break up any large air pockets. Bake for 45 minutes. When cake is cooked, invert tin and allow the cake to hang while it is cooling.

1 Sift together flour and cornflour, three times, then sift once again with $^1/_4$ cup/ 60 g/2 oz caster sugar.

2 Place egg whites, salt, cream of tartar and water in a large bowl and beat until stiff peaks form. Take care that you do not beat until the mixture is dry. Beat in vanilla essence, then fold in remaining caster sugar, 1 tablespoon at a time.

3 Sift flour mixture over egg white mixture then gently fold in. Lastly sprinkle shredded coconut over top of batter and fold in. Spoon batter into an ungreased angel food cake tin, then draw a spatula gently through the mixture to

4 To make frosting, place water and sugar in a saucepan and cook over a medium heat, without boiling, stirring constantly until sugar dissolves. Brush any sugar from sides of tin using a pastry brush dipped in water. Bring the syrup to the boil and boil rapidly for 3-5 minutes, without stirring, or until syrup reaches the soft-ball stage (115°C/239°F on a sugar thermometer). Place egg whites in a bowl and beat until soft peaks form. Continue to beat while pouring in syrup in a thin stream, a little at a time. Continue beating until all syrup is used and frosting stands in stiff peaks. Spread frosting over top and sides of cake and press toasted coconut onto sides of cake.

Serves 12

An angel cake tin is a deep-sided ring tin with a removable base that has a centre tube higher than the outside edges. If you do not have one of these tins you can use an ordinary deep-sided ring tin with a removable base. However, when you invert the tin for the cake to cool, place the tube over a funnel or bottle. Never grease an angel cake tin as this will stop the cake rising.

Coconut Angel Food Cake

RICH CHRISTMAS CAKE

250 g/8 oz sultanas
250 g/8 oz currants
250 g/8 oz raisins
125 g/4 oz mixed peel
250 g/8 oz glacé cherries, chopped
60 g/2 oz glacé pineapple, chopped
60 g/2 oz pitted dried dates, chopped
$^{1}/_{2}$ cup/125 mL/4 fl oz brandy
250 g/8 oz butter, softened
1 cup/170 g/5$^{1}/_{2}$ oz brown sugar
5 eggs
60 g/2 oz dark chocolate, melted
and cooled
1 teaspoon vanilla essence
1 teaspoon almond essence
2 teaspoons glycerine
2 tablespoons raspberry jam
1 teaspoon finely grated lemon rind
2 tablespoons lemon juice
2 cups/250 g/8 oz flour
1 teaspoon ground mixed spice
1 teaspoon ground ginger
$^{1}/_{4}$ teaspoon salt

FRUIT AND NUT TOPPING
2 tablespoons apricot jam
90 g/3 oz pecan or walnut halves
90 g/3 oz brazil nuts
60 g/2 oz blanched almonds
60 g/2 oz red glacé cherries
60 g/2 oz green glacé cherries

To line the cake tin, use a double-thickness folded strip of brown paper 5 cm/2 in higher than the cake tin and long enough to fit around the tin to overlap by about 2.5 cm/1 in. On the folded edge turn up about 2.5 cm/1 in and crease, then using scissors snip at regular intervals across the margin as far as the crease. Cut a piece of nonstick baking paper in the same way. Cut out a piece of brown paper and a piece of nonstick baking paper to fit the base of the tin. Grease the tin and place the strip of brown paper inside the tin with the snipped margin lying flat on the base of the tin. Ensure that the ends overlap so that the sides are completely covered by the paper. Repeat the process using the strip of baking paper. Place the base piece of brown paper, then the baking paper in the tin to cover the snipped margin.

1 Place sultanas, currants, raisins, mixed peel, chopped cherries, pineapple and dates in a bowl. Pour over 4 tablespoons brandy and toss to combine. Cover and stand overnight.

2 Lightly grease a 20 cm/8 in round or square cake tin and line base and sides of tin with brown paper, then with nonstick baking or greaseproof paper.

3 Place butter in a large bowl and beat until light and fluffy. Gradually add brown sugar, beating well after each addition.

Add eggs one at a time, beating well after each addition. Stir in chocolate, vanilla essence, almond essence, glycerine, jam, lemon rind and lemon juice.

4 Sift together flour, mixed spice, ginger and salt. Stir flour mixture and fruit mixture, alternately, into butter mixture and mix well to combine.

5 Spoon batter into prepared tin and smooth top. Drop tin onto a flat surface to break up any air bubbles and cook for 3-3$^{1}/_{2}$ hours or until cooked when tested with a skewer. Remove cake from oven, sprinkle with remaining brandy and set aside to cool in tin. When completely cold remove cake from tin. If you are

planning to store the cake, leave the paper on, wrap cake in a double thickness of foil and store in an airtight container.

6 To decorate, place jam in a small saucepan and heat, stirring over a low heat until melted, then push through a sieve. Brush top of cake with warm jam and then, using the picture as a guide, arrange pecans or walnuts, brazil nuts, almonds and cherries in an attractive pattern.

Makes a 20 cm/8 in round or square cake

Rich Christmas Cake

PALMIERS

170 g/5^1/$_2$ oz prepared puff pastry
15 g/^{1}/$_2$ oz butter, melted and cooled
3 tablespoons demerara sugar

3 Cut pastry length into eighteen slices and place on a greased baking tray. Flatten slightly and bake for 10-15 minutes or until puffed and golden.

The secret to making these heart-shaped pastries is in the way that you fold the pastry. Palmiers are a great way to use leftover puff pastry.

1 Roll out pastry to a 25 cm/10 in square, 3 mm/^{1}/$_8$ in thick.

Makes 18

2 Brush pastry with butter and sprinkle with a little sugar. Fold two opposite edges of pastry halfway towards the centre. Sprinkle with a little more sugar and fold one half of pastry over the other half. Press lightly to join.

VARIATIONS

Pistachio Palmiers: Combine 15 g/^{1}/$_2$ oz finely chopped unsalted pistachio nuts and 3 tablespoons brown sugar and sprinkle over pastry in place of demerara sugar.

Almond Palmiers: Combine 3 tablespoons ground almonds, 2 tablespoons caster sugar and 1 teaspoon ground mixed spice and sprinkle over pastry in place of demerara sugar.

Try sandwiching the Palmiers together with whipped cream. Delicious!

Palmiers

GINGERBREAD HOUSE

Oven temperature
180°C, 350°F, Gas 4

6 cups/750 g/1$^{1}/_{2}$ lb self-raising flour
4 teaspoons ground mixed spice
pinch salt
$^{1}/_{2}$ cup/170 g/5$^{1}/_{2}$ oz honey
2 cups/350 g/11 oz brown sugar
90 g/3 oz butter
2 eggs, beaten
2 teaspoons finely grated lemon rind
2 tablespoons lemon juice

ROYAL ICING
4 egg whites
1 kg/2 lb icing sugar, sifted
2 teaspoons lemon juice
2 teaspoons glycerine

DECORATIONS
1 packet clear fruit drops
20 long, thin crisp chocolate mint sticks
1 packet fruit jellies
1 packet candy-coated chocolate drops
22 walnut halves
14 blanched almonds
2 chocolate flake bars

3   Make a well in the centre of flour mixture, pour in honey mixture, add eggs, lemon rind and lemon juice and mix to form a soft dough. Turn dough onto a lightly floured surface and knead until smooth. Divide dough into three equal portions. Roll out each portion to fit a greased and lined 26 x 32 cm/10$^{1}/_{2}$ x 12$^{3}/_{4}$ in Swiss roll tin and bake for 20-25 minutes or until lightly browned.

4   Using the pattern, cut out paper templates. While dough is still warm, cut out shapes. Leave gingerbread in tin to cool.

1   Sift together flour, mixed spice and salt into a large bowl and set aside.

2   Place honey, sugar and butter in a saucepan and cook over a low heat, stirring, until all ingredients are melted and combined. Remove from heat and set aside to cool slightly.

If you only have one Swiss roll tin, bake one gingerbread slab at a time.

Gingerbread House

5 To make icing, place egg whites in a bowl and beat until foamy. Gradually beat in icing sugar, lemon juice and glycerine to make a stiff icing.

6 Using icing to secure, assemble house as follows. Secure support pieces about 5 mm/¼ in from each corner of end panels. Fix end panel and side panels together, holding firmly in place for a few seconds to secure. Place on a lined cake board.

7 Spread a little icing over one side panel. Secure clear fruit drops in each window frame. Cut mint sticks to fit top and bottom of windows. Decorate with fruit jellies, candy-coated chocolate drops and walnut halves. Repeat on second side.

8 Decorate front and end panels in a similar way. Decorate corners with almonds. Fix roof panels in position.

'To be able to cut cooked dough into shapes without hurrying, stagger baking times by placing tins in oven at 10-minute intervals.'

9 Stick chimney pieces together and fix in position on roof. Cover roof with icing. Decorate with clear fruit drops and candy-coated chocolate drops.

10 Spread icing over Christmas trees and fix in position.

11 Cut chocolate flake bars to resemble logs and place in position. Leave house overnight to dry.

Makes 1 house

'Cover Royal Icing with a clean damp teatowel to prevent it drying out when not using.'

Figure 1

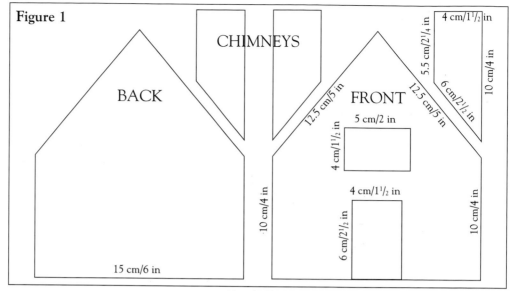

CHIMNEYS

BACK

FRONT

4 cm/1½ in

5.5 cm/2¼ in

12.5 cm/5 in

12.5 cm/5 in

6 cm/2½ in

10 cm/4 in

5 cm/2 in

4 cm/1½ in

4 cm/1½ in

6 cm/2½ in

10 cm/4 in

10 cm/4 in

15 cm/6 in

32 cm/12¾ in

Figure 2

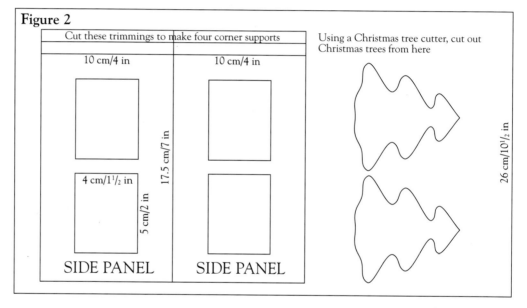

Cut these trimmings to make four corner supports

Using a Christmas tree cutter, cut out Christmas trees from here

10 cm/4 in

10 cm/4 in

17.5 cm/7 in

4 cm/1½ in

5 cm/2 in

SIDE PANEL

SIDE PANEL

26 cm/10½ in

Figure 3

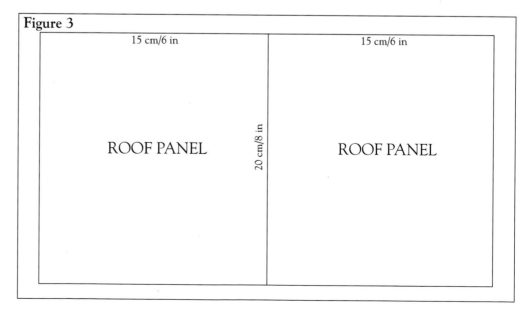

15 cm/6 in

15 cm/6 in

ROOF PANEL

20 cm/8 in

ROOF PANEL

CHOCOLATE PINWHEELS

125 g/4 oz butter
²/₃ cup/140 g/4¹/₂ oz caster sugar
1 teaspoon vanilla essence
1 egg
1³/₄ cups/220 g/7 oz flour
¹/₄ cup/30 g/1 oz cocoa powder

Oven temperature
180°C, 350°F, Gas 4

1 Place butter, sugar and vanilla essence in a bowl and beat until mixture is creamy. Add egg and beat until well combined.

3 Roll out each portion between two sheets of greaseproof paper to form a 20 x 30 cm/8 x 12 in rectangle. Remove top sheet of paper from each and invert one onto the other. Roll up from longer edge to form a long roll. Wrap in plastic food wrap and refrigerate for 1 hour.

4 Cut roll into 5 mm/¹/₄ in slices, place on greased baking trays and bake for 10-12 minutes or until lightly browned. Cool on wire racks.

Makes 30

These are ideal last-minute biscuits. The dough can be made in advance and kept in the refrigerator until needed.

2 Divide mixture into two equal portions. Sift 1 cup/125 g/4 oz flour into one portion and mix to combine. Sift together cocoa powder and remaining flour and mix into other portion.

THE ESSENTIAL INGREDIENTS

The three most important ingredients you use when making wonderful home-baked goodies are sugar, flour and shortening. Each plays an important role in the finished cake or biscuit. Understanding how they work will ensure that you get the results that will make you want to bake and bake again.

SWEETENERS

The earliest sweeteners were honey, sweet fruits, and syrups extracted from fruit. These are still used, but by far the most popular sweetener today is white table sugar. In baking, sugar acts not only as a sweetener, but also helps to produce a soft, spongy texture and improves the keeping quality of cakes.

CASTER SUGAR: Caster sugar is the best white sugar for making cakes as it dissolves quickly and easily.

GRANULATED SUGAR: Granulated sugar is coarser than caster sugar and although it is often used in cake-making it can result in a cake with a slightly reduced volume and a speckled crust.

BROWN SUGAR: Brown sugar can be used in place of caster sugar, however it gives a richer flavour and colour to the cake.

ICING SUGAR: Icing sugar is not usually used in cake-making, as it gives a cake poor volume and a hard crust. It is, however, ideal for icings.

☙ In cakes that use the melt-and-mix method – the melted fat and sugar mixture is added to the dry ingredients – granulated, raw or demerara sugars can be used, as the sugar is dissolved before baking.

☙ Honey adds a distinctive flavour to baked products and makes them dense and moist with better keeping qualities.

☙ If using honey in place of sugar, reduce the amount of honey used by one-quarter and bake at a slightly lower temperature. Baked products made with honey brown more quickly than those made with sugar.

Flour

Flour provides the structure that holds the cake together. The most common flour is that milled from wheat, but there are also other flours that can be used in baking to give interesting and varying results.

FLOUR: This is a blend of hard and soft wheat flours. The proportions tend to vary a little from country to country. For example in America, where flour is known as all-purpose flour, the proportion of hard wheat flour is usually greater than in flours produced in Europe. The American cake flour and pastry flours are soft wheat flours.

SELF-RAISING FLOUR: This is flour with baking powder and salt added. You can make your own self-raising flour if you wish by sifting flour with baking powder – for 1 cup/125 g/4 oz flour allow 1 teaspoon baking powder.

WHOLEMEAL FLOUR: This flour uses the whole grain so retains all the flavour and nutrients of the grain. Wholemeal flour has a higher bran content than white flour which reduces the effectiveness of the gluten. Therefore, baked goods made with wholemeal flour tend to have a heavier, more dense texture.

᛫ Sifting flour is important as it adds air to the mixture, giving lightness to your baked products. To sift flour, hold the sieve well above the bowl so the flour gets a good airing as it falls into the bowl.

᛫ Flour should be stored in an airtight container in a cool, dark place. Due to its moisture and fat content flour will eventually go rancid.

Shortenings

᛫ Fat or shortening in whatever form makes a cake tender and helps improve the keeping quality.

᛫ Good quality margarine and butter are usually interchangeable.

᛫ In most cases fats should be at room temperature for cake- and biscuit-making. To allow hard shortenings to soften, stand at room temperature for an hour before using.

᛫ If using a soft margarine high in polyunsaturated fats, use it straight from the refrigerator.

᛫ Oil is sometimes used in baked products. This is a lighter alternative to butter or margarine and is often used in recipes for carrot cake.

᛫ If using an oil for making a cake, choose one that has a mild flavour. Corn and vegetable oils are good choices.

Never use olive oil or other strong-flavoured oil or your cake will have an unpleasant flavour.

᛫ Butter absorbs other smells easily, so when keeping it in the refrigerator make sure that it is covered and away from ingredients such as onions and fish, or you will have a strong-smelling butter that can affect the taste of baked goods.

᛫ Butter keeps well in the freezer for up to three months, if well wrapped.

᛫ As oils have a tendency to turn rancid quickly they should be stored away from heat and light. The refrigerator is a good place to store oils. You will find that some oils go cloudy and semi-solid when stored in the refrigerator, but will quickly revert to their original state when left at room temperature for a short time.

INDEX

UK COOKERY EDITOR
Katie Swallow

EDITORIAL
Food Editor: Rachel Blackmore
Editorial Assistant: Ella Martin
Editorial Coordinator: Margaret Kelly
Recipe Development: Sheryle Eastwood, Lucy Kelly, Donna Hay,
Anneka Mitchell, Penelope Peel, Belinda Warn, Loukie Werle
Credits: Recipe page 70 Pat Alburey © Merehurst Limited

COVER
Photography: Ashley Mackevicius
Styling: Wendy Berecry

PHOTOGRAPHY
Ashley Mackevicius, Harm Mol, Yanto Noerianto, Andy Payne,
Jon Stewart, Warren Webb

STYLING
Wendy Berecry, Belinda Clayton, Rosemary De Santis, Carolyn
Fienberg, Jacqui Hing, Michelle Gorry

DESIGN AND PRODUCTION
Manager: Sheridan Carter
Layout: Lulu Dougherty
Finished Art: Stephen Joseph
Design: Frank Pithers

Published by J.B. Fairfax Press Pty Limited
A.C.N. 003 738 430
Formatted by J.B. Fairfax Press Pty Limited
Output by Adtype, Sydney
Printed by Toppan Printing Co, Singapore

Includes Index
ISBN 1 86343 101 2 (pbk)

Distributed by J.B. Fairfax Press Limited
9 Trinity Centre, Park Farm Estate
Wellingborough, Northants
Ph: (0933) 402330 Fax: (0933) 402234